The
Rose Growers
Handbook

Janet Cheriton

David Bateman

This book is dedicated to my sons, Mark and David

Published in 1992 by David Bateman Ltd., 'Golden Heights', 32-34 View Road, Glenfield, Auckland, New Zealand

ISBN 1 86953 108 6

Cover by Big Red Design
Typeset in 10.5/12 Palatino
Printed in Hong Kong by Colorcraft Ltd

Contents

Acknowledgements

There are many people whose help has been invaluable in the writing of this book. I want to thank all of them for their assistance, and for giving so generously of their time to advise me in their various areas of expertise.

Mr Travis Flint, immediate past President of the Auckland Rose Society and past Vice President of the National Rose Society of New Zealand, whose help has been unstinting and ongoing.

Mr Allan Scott, M.B.E., A.H.R.I.H., President Emeritus of the National Rose Society; a man for whom nothing is too much trouble, and whose wisdom and love of roses is inspirational. The rose nurseries of Frank Mason and Son, Swane Bros., Tasman Bay Roses, Egmont Roses, Rasmussens Roses and Riverland Nurseries for their generous help with the lists of recommended cultivars. Ian Duncalf of Parva Plants for his advice and suggestions for companion plants and interplanting.

Brian Callaghan of Lifetech laboratories, for explaining the intricacies of tissue culture of roses.

Judy King of Balclutha for sharing her garden with me by mail over a long correspondence.

Emma Harding for reading the manuscript and suggesting changes from a non-rosarian's point of view.

The many members of Rose Societies, who have shared with me their accumulated knowledge about roses and their culture; especially Mary Weal, Cyril Baber, Judy Haigh and Ken Rose (Auckland), Moira Sligo (Oamaru), Mrs Noel Simpson, Dorothy Miller and Jean Brown (Dunedin) and Dot Turner (Franklin).

Thanks also to all of those rosarians in Australia who helped in so many ways, and whose friendship makes rose growing even more of a joy.

Thanks must go, too, to my husband John who drew the diagrams that clarify so many points in the text, and who is unendingly patient and supportive.

Janet Cheriton

Author's preface

On reading any of the rose books owned by our parents, and often emanating from the United Kingdom, we could be forgiven for thinking that roses are petulant 'prima donnas' that must be treated 'just so'. Nothing could be further from the truth! The *real* truth, happily, is well and truly out; roses are ridiculously easy to grow.

Moreover, in the Southern Hemisphere, we have the benefit of relatively mild climates and our roses can bloom for most of the year.

With the addition of just a little knowledge about roses' cultural needs, and a little experience too, we can all grow wonderful roses. With roses, as with other plants, it is not so much a matter of how much you do, but how much you know.

This book aims to simplify and 'de-mystify' many aspects of rose growing in the hope that many more gardeners and, indeed, non-gardeners will feel greater confidence in their ability to grow this 'Queen of Flowers'. If the book can also extend the interests of more experienced rose growers, then it will have well and truly achieved its aim.

Janet Cheriton

Foreword

The rose is unquestionably the most loved of all flowers and due mainly to the interest created in the 'Queen of Flowers' by the National Rose Society of New Zealand (Inc) and its many affiliated District Rose Societies, the love of the rose has now expanded even wider.

New growers will find established rosarians approachable, helpful, friendly and very informative. One only has to drive around our country, both north and south, to realise that in most of our New Zealand soils, and with our favourable climatic conditions, roses can be grown to perfection.

This handbook, therefore, is a timely publication and, using the cultural methods advocated by the author to grow roses, gardeners will be well rewarded for their efforts. This book covers all aspects of rose culture for the novice gardener and the more experienced devotee; both will find in these pages a wealth of information that will guide them to success with any or all of the rose cultivars now available in New Zealand.

Allan G. Scott   M.B.E., A.H.R.I.H., N.Z.R.A., S.M.A.

Introduction

This old world we're livin' in
Is might hard to beat;
You get a thorn with every rose,
But ain't the roses sweet.

Anon

The rose is undoubtedly the most loved and widely cultivated flower in the world; one reason for this is its ease of cultivation and adaptability to most climates and soil types. Whether in vast, rambling gardens or small pots on balconies, the rose reigns supreme for beauty and fragrance, and it is, moreover, a plant that is remarkably hardy and enormously rewarding to grow. There are varieties to scramble up trees, climb fences or pergolas, provide low-growing borders or hedges, and to suit any other situation that a gardener might require. Yet in all of its variations, the rose remains identifiably itself; beautiful, usually fragrant and free blooming, with each cultivar (cultivated variety) possessing its own unique form. Whether your patch of soil is large or minute, there are roses to complement it ... indeed the rose is the flower for all gardens.

As fossil remains prove, there were roses in the Northern Hemisphere millions of years ago. That the genus has continued to survive and prosper until now is an indication of the plant's hardiness and adaptability. The rose is mentioned in Greek mythology and Roman legend, and the historian Herodotus (BC 484-424) wrote that it was grown in the legendary gardens of King Midas. It was ultimately through the Christian faith that the rose was carried across Europe and to the West, with the five wounds of Christ being said to be represented by the five petals of the rose.

Of course this historic five-petalled rose is very different from most of the modern rose cultivars that we know today, but today's gardeners may, if they choose, grow these five-petalled forebears of modern roses. This is one of the great joys of rose growing; that so many ancient varieties have been preserved and may be grown for their historical significance, their long association with people, as well as for the other virtues they possess.

It is not the function of this book to deal in detail with the history of the rose, as that has been capably done elsewhere (see Bibliography), but it may be of interest to the reader to know that the rose and mankind have come a long way together. The rose is very much a part of our lives and a part of our history, yet new variations of the genus *Rosa* are constantly being raised all over the world to further enchant and delight us.

The rose is a flower of which one will never tire; it is revered for its history, loved for its beauty and fragrance, admired for its versatility and adaptability, and grown in whatever patch of soil you call your garden.

1 Site

He who would grow beautiful roses in his garden
must have beautiful roses in his heart
Dean Hole

There are no secrets to growing good garden roses. However, there are some necessities of life for the rose, and these must be provided if roses are to perform at their best. Attention must be paid to siting the plants with a view to obtaining maximum sunshine, adequate drainage, good air circulation, sufficient water, protection from strong winds and the proper nutrients. Given all of these basic requirements, roses will flourish and grow in any soil type.

Sun

Roses love the sun. Without it they will droop miserably, flower sparsely (if at all) and fall prey to a multitude of diseases. While you may be able to manipulate your roses' soil, drainage, access to water, food and wind protection, you must give your first consideration to a sunny site. This is one of the few aspects of rose culture on which all rose growers agree, so make it your first priority. Select a site that gets a minimum of five hours of sun each day; more if possible.

Drainage

Roses cannot live with their roots in water. Good drainage is absolutely essential. If your selected site does not already have good drainage, then you must take steps to provide it. Possibly the simplest and least expensive way to do this is by raising the level of the rose beds by the addition of good topsoil on top of the existing beds in order to create a topsoil depth of around 30 cm. You can retain this soil in the beds by means of a low wall of rocks, a concrete edging or low-growing ground cover plants which will prevent the soil from washing down to the lower level in heavy rain.

To test if your soil is likely to become waterlogged in heavy rain, dig a hole about 30 cm deep and fill it with water. If the water does not drain away after 12 hours, then you are likely to have a problem in a wet season. So raise the bed as suggested above, slope the bed gently, or consider the other option, a drainage system.

Drains can be made of terracotta, earthenware or plastic, the latter being cheap and readily available. Laying a drainage system can be a time-consuming task, but it is essential where a raised bed is not an alternative. If you recoil at the thought of laying drains, then seek professional help. If tackling the job yourself, remember that the water you drain from the rose beds will flow to the lowest point that it can, so make sure that you have made provision for this, or you could end up with a swamp where you least expected it, or worse ... your neighbour could end up with one! But on the bright side, a swampy area in a garden is no bad thing and there are many plants that relish such an environment. You could always buy a *Gunnera manicata*, a giant Amazonian jungle plant that resembles a huge, prickly rhubarb. Feed it well and watch in wonder as it grows to a spectacular size.

Another drainage problem that is more easily solved is that of little or very poor topsoil over heavy clay. In such cases, rotary hoeing will begin to solve the problem, but do not hoe too deeply or you will lose what topsoil you have. Then add some gypsum or a proprietary clay breaker to make the clay more friable. More topsoil can then be added with liberal quantities of mulch material which will rot down and further improve the soil.

All of this, of course, should be carried out some months before planting the roses, so that the topsoil and mulch material have had time to be incorporated into the soil . Digging over several times, over three or four months will further aerate the soil and hasten the breaking down of the mulch materials.

Air

Roses like to be grown where air can circulate freely. This helps the plants to remain free of fungus diseases that may occur if they are crowded together. It is also wise to avoid sites where the overhang of eaves will prevent the free circulation of air through the plants. The roots, too, need ventilation and this is best provided by a friable, crumbly textured soil. If this is not provided, then soil bacteria cannot work and carbon dioxide cannot escape from the soil.

Water

Roses love plenty of water in order to be at their best, but, as previously stated, they will not survive with 'wet feet' on a permanent basis. Water should be able to percolate gently downward through the soil, carrying essential nutrients to the roots, and then it should be able to drain away. In dry situations, or in sandy soil, it will be necessary to augment natural rainfall in order to help the plants obtain the nourishment they need through their root system. In many areas, watering will only be needed during dry spells, and a trickle irrigation system is useful if you have a number of beds to attend to.

Overhead watering is widely practised in summer, but it is not without its problems. Many growers consider that it spreads fungus disease, particularly black spot. This seems to hold true if watering is done later in the day, creating high humidity and allowing the leaves to remain wet for five or six hours or overnight. So when planning overhead watering, try to do it early enough in the day so that the foliage has dried before nightfall.

Like a good shower of rain, a good, deep watering can only benefit rose plants, but the key word here is 'deep'. It is worse than useless to sprinkle the roses lightly, even on a regular basis. This wetting of just the top layer of soil does not allow the water to percolate down to the roots, and in fact will only encourage the roses to send their roots into this surface area where they will quickly dry out and die in the next hot spell. So a casual, light sprinkling is out, however picturesque it may feel to wander aimlessly about with a hand-held hose on hot summer evenings! Watering deeply and far less often is the standard rule of thumb for roses, and in fact most other plants, too.

A thick organic mulch on the beds will help to conserve water lost by evaporation in the summer and will have the added advantage of keeping the beds free of competing weeds.

Shelter

Although roses are sturdy plants, they need shelter from strong winds, particularly when newly planted, as the roots have not yet had a chance to anchor the plants firmly in the ground. Roses will tolerate a great deal of adverse weather, but strong winds will rock the plants to and fro, tearing constantly at their roots and weakening their grip in the soil. Standard roses, being budded higher, are particularly prone to wind damage and should always be staked in windy areas. Bush and shrub roses are less likely to suffer from this kind of damage, but it is as well to stake them when they are first planted out, and to tie them firmly to prevent rocking of the roots in the wind. If a light shelter can be arranged in the form of an open trellis or a windbreak planting of shrubs, so much the better, but keep in mind the importance of sunlight to the roses and do not build or plant a wind screen that blocks out the sun.

Competition

Roses are greedy feeders and so will not thrive where there is strong competition for food from large trees, shrubs or hedges, especially when they are young plants and the trees and shrubs are established. Of course, roses can be grown with other plants, and this can be to their mutual benefit, but keep in mind the food needs of the roses and do not force them to share the same ground with large, established trees.

There are some rose cultivars that will romp happily up trees, but these should be planted with their roots some distance from the trunk to allow the roses to establish themselves away from competitionfrom the tree's roots, or plant the rose well inside the drip line of the tree, outside of which line is where the tree's feeder roots will be. In both cases, you will need to feed the rose well for the first year or two.

2 Soil

So if you want to live again
Try digging in the soil.
Plant yourself a rose bush
And triumph from your toil.

Helen M. Zechella

We are fortunate that roses will grow in nearly all soil types and techniques for preparing soil vary from the 'purist' who will prepare his or her beds months before planting and solemnly turn them on a monthly basis, to the 'impulse buyer' who, falling for a pot grown rose in a garden centre, will scratch out a small depression in the soil and hurl the rose unceremoniously into it. Both gardeners will ultimately have blooms, proving just how adaptable roses are. However, to the purist I would suggest that it doesn't have to be that laborious and to the impulse buyer that just a little effort will reward you a hundredfold.

The soil in which you plant your roses has two separate functions. It provides an anchor for the plant, to hold it firmly in place against the vagaries of the weather, and it is the medium through which the plant gains its nutrients, which are in soluble form in the soil's moisture.

There are two aspects of the soil with which you must concern yourself; these are **condition** and **content.** Condition is the structure of the soil, whether sand, clay, loam or somewhere in between. Content is the amount and type of nutrients contained in the soil, and their availability to the plants' roots. Both condition and content may be altered, so there is no need to despair if your soil does not come up to the 'deep, rich loam' often advocated. By understanding the functions of the soil in relation to roses, it is possible to manipulate your patch of earth into the perfect environment for your plants.

Condition

Firstly, what sort of soil do you already have? Is it light and sandy? Solid, heavy clay? Or deep volcanic loam? If the latter, I suggest that you skip this chapter entirely, as you will have no need for advice on how to manipulate *your soil*. For intending rose growers, however, with sandy, pumice, peat or clay soil, solutions to the problem are possible.

Sandy soil needs the incorporation of a great deal of organic matter, and this may include commercially prepared compost, manures of all types, grass clippings, leaf mould, wood ash, tan bark or anything else of animal or vegetable origin that you can obtain, by purchase, making or scrounging from friends and neighbours. Yes, you *can* just throw all of this without ceremony on to your proposed rose bed, but it is better to first shred, mix and age the material before applying it to the bed. This will allow for faster decomposition and incorporation into the soil.

If you don't have access to a shredder and can't bear to wait for the material to age, add a liberal quantity of blood and bone which will help to speed breakdown and also prevent the process of decomposition from using up all the nitrogen in the soil. Water the mixture in well and keep it damp but not sodden, turning it every month or two to aerate.

The main problem with sandy soil is that it does not retain nutrients or water, so both its condition *and content* need to be improved if roses are to succeed. Sand will not absorb water, which passes through, wetting only the outer edge of each granule. **Pumice soils** will absorb some moisture and retain it for a period, but, like sandy soil, it requires large amounts of humus to be added over a long period, with phosphate and blood and bone. When ample water is available, pumice soils will grow splendid roses. Note, however, that cobalt, an essential plant nutrient, is often missing in pumice soils.

Peat soils will also grow excellent roses. Initially, the peat soil needs to be treated with lime and basic slag, which is the dross from iron works in powdered form. It contains mostly iron, but also minute amounts of trace elements, including calcium. Heavy dressings of phosphate and potash should also be incorporated before planting roses in such soil. In drought conditions, if peaty soil becomes completely dry it is extremely difficult to get water to penetrate it again; sometimes it can take a whole winter to get the peat soil wet enough to support good growth.

Clay soils hold a great deal of water, but in solid clay, where the clay particles are bound tightly together, the water, and thus the nutrients it contains, are not available to the roses' roots. Fortunately it is possible to purchase products that will improve clay soils. They are a combination of peat and fine bark, compost and dolomite lime, and need only to be forked in lightly and left to do their work in breaking up the clay.

Clay soils also benefit from large amounts of organic matter, preferably composted first, and gypsum (calcium sulphate) can be added to alter the condition of the clay, rendering it more fertile and friable. Incorporate the organic matter by digging it in if you are able to do so, but even if it is laid thickly on the top of the bed as a mulch and receives a reasonable amount of rain over a period of months, the condition of the soil will improve.

Bear in mind that the roses you plant may live over 20 years, perhaps more. A huge Banksia rose in Tombstone, Arizona, apparently planted in 1885, now covers an area of over 600 square metres and 150 people may sit under its branches! This is the only chance you will get to the prepare the site for your roses, so the time and effort you put into this initial preparation will be well worth it in terms of future blooming.

After adding to the soil, allow it to settle and consolidate. If possible, give it an occasional loose forking over to further incorporate the organic matter and to remove weeds that germinate. This forking will also help to aerate the soil. It is not necessary to add artificial fertilisers at this stage, provided that enough humus has been included.

The depth of suitable soil for roses is important. The soil needs to be deep enough for the roses' roots to anchor the plant firmly and it needs to sustain the plant with food. It is of little use planting your rose so that its roots are in the lower subsoil without access to nutrients. Make your topsoil as deep as possible, at least 30 cm to ensure successful anchoring and feeding. Remember that it is the *roots* of the plant that must be in good soil, so allow for this in your preparation.

Content

There are two types of fertilisers. The first, organic fertilisers, are composed of rotted-down animal and vegetable wastes, e.g., manures and composts of all types. The second type, inorganic fertilisers, are manufactured from chemicals in proportions suitable for the growing needs of specific plants, e.g., superphosphate and proprietary rose foods. The rose will not distinguish between fertilisers of either type, as long as its nutrient needs are being met, but from a soil condition point of view, organic fertilisers are to be preferred if available, as inorganic fertilisers may have a detrimental effect on soil bacteria and earthworm populations if used exclusively without the addition from time to time of organic matter.

Fortunately, most New Zealand and Australian soils are slightly acid and this suits roses very well. Soils range from acid to alkaline and their acidity or alkalinity is measured on a scale called the pH scale, with a neutral reading being pH 7. Acidity is indicated by a lower number and alkalinity by a higher number. Roses will grow well in soils with a reading around pH 6.5 to pH 8.5, so there is probably no need to even consider this issue in your garden, as humus-enriched soil is almost certain to be within the acceptable range preferred by roses. However, if you would *like* to check your soil's pH level, test kits are available.

For the record, strongly acid soil can be made more alkaline by the addition of lime and strongly alkaline soil can be remedied by the addition of peat and/or sulphur. Do consult a local rose society however, before purchasing truckloads of any of these chemicals, as getting the soil 'just right' can prove obsessive to the point where you never actually grow any roses at all!

Within the preferred pH range, all the necessary nutrients will most likely be available to the plants. If a deficiency exists in a particular area, the local rose society will know about it and will be able to advise you on how to correct the problem. In some areas phosphorus may be lacking, but it is probably best to assume that if the garden grows other plants or even weeds well, then it will grow roses well, too. Build up your soil with as much humus as you can find, incorporate it as well as you are able, then let the rain and the earthworms do the rest.

Trace elements are only needed in minute quantities and are usually contained in most garden soils. Most commercial rose foods also contain all of these elements. If trace elements are lacking in your soil, they will *not* be added by using home-made compost, as the vegetable matter you use will also be lacking in that element, so the deficiency will need to be made good by inorganic fertilisers and other additives according to the nature of the deficiency.

Nutritional deficiency symptoms and how to correct them

Symptoms	Deficiency	Apply to correct
Foliage pale green, small flowers, poor growth	Nitrogen	Blood and bone Manure

Symptoms	Deficiency	Apply to correct
Pale leaves, red to bronzing.	Phosphate	Blood and bone Superphosphate
Leaves brown, look scorched on tips and edges. Poor growth.	Potassium	Wood ash Manure, compost
Edge of leaves brown, curl and dry up. Centres of leaves still green.	Calcium	Gypsum, bone meal Basic slag Superphosphate.
Yellow/purple leaves with green veins.	Magnesium	Basic slag, fish meal Epsom salts
Pale foliage with yellow veins.	Sulphur	Ammonium sulphate Potassium sulphate
Pale foliage with green veins, yellow stems.	Iron	Bone meal, dried blood, basic slag
New foliage malformed, may yellow or mottle	Boron	Fish meal, soot Powdered borax
Pale spots usually on older leaves, some mottling	Manganese	Manganese sulphate Sewage, sludge
Pale, thick leaves, top growth does not develop	Zinc, copper molybdenum	Sewage sludge, zinc sulphate, copper sulphate, sodium, molybdate

Humus is the key word in the feeding of roses. Unless there is sufficient humus incorporated into the soil of rose beds, then feeding with chemical fertilisers is useless, for if the condition of the soil is not right, then the plants are unable to take up the nutrients in the fertilisers. It is best for the new grower of roses to look first to the condition and content of the soil, relying solely on enrichment with humus, and learning more about the roses' specific needs before swamping them with expensive and unnecessary chemicals which may well result in rank growth and poor quality blooms. Blood and bone is a completely safe, slow-acting general purpose fertiliser which can be used in moderation; say 50 grams per plant applied in late winter, incorporated into the soil or used as a top dressing when feeding is required again in spring. It must be stressed, however, that *no* nutrients can be absorbed by the plants unless in solution in water; it is water that carries these nutrients to the plants.

If you are planning just a few roses, or perhaps roses in pots, and don't feel inclined to go to great lengths to improve the condition and content of a large area of garden all at once, there is a simple alternative. If you have purchased the roses, either as 'bare root' plants in winter or 'pot grown' at any time of the year, you need only also purchase a quantity of 'planting mix' or 'tree and shrub mix', both of which are packed in bags for convenience. Dig the holes for the roses twice or three times as wide and deep as you think the rose will need, half fill the prepared mix, then plant the rose (see Chapter 4), filling in around the roots with more of the mix, firming it down and watering well. A further layer of the mix laid on top of the soil will provide a temporary mulch, and because such mixes contain all of the required nutrients, your roses should thrive until it is time to feed them again.

This is a short cut and must be seen as such, but it does provide an alternative to the greater amount of work required in preparing a large section of garden. Feeding and maintenance should be carried out routinely for roses planted in this way, as for roses planted in well prepared soil. Be warned though that rose growing is highly addictive, and it is likely that your 'just a few' roses may well multiply very quickly into a hundred or more in a very short space of time.

On-going feeding

There are all sorts of fads and fashions about rose feeding, and any number of proprietary brands of 'complete rose food' from which to choose. But it should be borne in mind that the rose has survived both with and without these 'miracle foods' for millions of years, showing once again the adaptability of the genus. There is, moreover, no one rose food that will satisfy the needs of growers everywhere, because, as mentioned earlier, soils differ in both their composition and content. The grower will soon become aware of the needs of his or her own roses after watching their performance for a season or two.

Plant foods are made up of many elements and most of the nutrients required by roses will be present in a well-made garden soil, enriched with well-rotted compost made from a large variety of plant and animal matter. Supplementary feeding at various times of the year (see Chapter 9) can be used, but with discretion. The major chemical elements of proprietary rose foods are nitrogen, phosphorus and potassium, denoted by the letters N:P:K, in that order, and it is the ratio of these elements to each other that is of major importance in rose feeding.

Nitrogen produces good growth and large foliage, and without sufficient nitrogen roses will grow poorly, with small flowers and leaves and weak stems. Phosphorus is needed for root growth in roses and helps to give the petals their firm texture. Roses deficient in phosphorus may drop their leaves and fail to make strong roots. Potassium is a general health food for roses, keeping them healthy and hardening the tissues of the plants, giving them greater disease resistance. Other minor chemical elements needed are magnesium, iron, cobalt, boron, sulphur and manganese and these, like the major elements of nitrogen, phosphorus and potassium, will usually be supplied abundantly by regular use of well-made compost.

Compost

Compost, when well made, can provide all the feeding needs of your roses, so it is worthwhile at this stage to give some thought to your future supply of compost, its making and its storage. As you will undoubtedly find, you can never have enough compost for all your gardening needs, and roses, being such greedy feeders, will use up large amounts of this valuable material.

A compost heap, or better two or three heaps, should be enclosed at the sides, but not at the bottom, for this is where the earthworms and soil bacteria can get in and do a great deal of the work, changing the material used into a good, rich mix suitable for use in the garden. Plastic compost bins are generally available, usually made of recycled plastics. These bins are also aesthetically more acceptable than an unsightly 'rubbish heap' at the bottom of the garden that is so often dignified with the title of 'compost heap'. Frequently, however, these bins do not contain sufficient air holes and so the home compost maker would be well advised to add a few more holes to help aerate the contents.

The wider the range of materials used in composting, the better the result will be, so use all possible vegetable waste ... lawn clippings, kitchen waste, leaves, dead flowers, prunings (but not from diseased plants!), untreated sawdust and wood shavings, tan bark, seaweed, shredded newspaper and so on. Animal manures can also be added to the compost mix whenever they are available. Track down a source of animal or fowl manure and investigate to see if your local council has a recycled garden waste by-product that can often be purchased at minimal cost to ratepayers of that district.

The heat generated in a compost heap or bin will usually be sufficient to kill most weed seeds, but avoid putting the determined types like oxalis into your heap. The mix should be built in layers where possible, layering, for example, lawn clippings over horse manure over soil over shredded prunings. A liberal sprinkling of blood and bone in the heap will help, too.

Having progessively filled your bin or built your heap to a size that is convenient for you, cover it, sprinkle occasionally with water to keep it moist and actively decomposing, then go away and start your next one. You can give the mix a stir or turn if you wish, as this will hasten the decomposition process. Come back in a few months, more or less according to the time of year, and give your compost the look, feel and smell test. Ready to use compost will be darkish brown, feel crumbly in your hands and have a pleasant, earthy smell like the floor of a forest. A little lime mixed in with the compost will correct the natural tendency of compost to be rather acidic. Wonderful stuff compost: the only real 'miracle food' for plants!

Foliar feeding

Foliar feeding of roses is a useful booster and many proprietary preparations are available. These contain most of the roses' needs in soluble form and are applied to the foliage via a spray. As the nutrients are in solution they are able to be taken up by the leaves. The rule here is to use the solution strictly in accordance with the directions, or even a little on the weaker side as a too strong mix can burn the leaves. It is often possible to mix the foliar feed in with your usual pest and disease spray, but *do* read the labels carefully before mixing what could be a potentially lethal feed for your roses! A large proportion of a roses' solid food needs are absorbed through their foliage from the atmosphere, so foliar feeding, with a suitable product, makes good sense as an adjunct to, but never a substitute for, your root feeding.

3 What kind of rose?

If I give you a rose, you will not doubt God any more.
Tertullian (c.160-225AD)

While selection of the kind of roses for any garden situation is very much a matter of personal choice, there are some kinds that are almost guaranteed to do exceptionally well in any part of the Southern Hemisphere. These are tried-and-true varieties that thousands of rose growers will endorse. Recommending different categories of roses is at best a risky business in a book such as this, and the intending grower would do well to consult the local rose society for the kinds of roses that do well in that area. Also, the catalogues from major nurseries make intriguing and exciting reading for all gardeners, and will give a reliable guide to the size of growth expected, flower description and fragrance.

Do bear in mind that all of these aspects of rose growing will vary throughout a country, depending on soil, climate and feeding, but local rosarians know this and will give generously of their time and experience to help you to choose roses that will give you years of pleasure. Don't, however, deprive yourself of the fun of growing some of the newer releases from time to time, as it is from these new roses that will come the top choices and 'old favourites' of subsequent years.

It may be wise to select a few trusted cultivars for a start, then, having gained confidence, try some of the new roses. Gardening magazines will be of great help to the new rose grower. Many have regular rose columns and often feature detailed articles about specific cultivars and how they flourish in different areas.

There are many different kinds of roses and it is worth some time to discover the attributes of each kind before deciding what to order.

Old-fashioned roses

Old-fashioned roses vary from enormous rambling types, that will cover a large wall in a season or two, to tiny dwarf growers suitable for

21

pot culture on even the smallest deck. In every garden there is room for at least one of these charming roses.

Many of the Old-fashioned roses are noted for their fragrance and others for the sheer beauty of their blooms. Most are also incredibly hardy plants, requiring almost no maintenance in the way of pruning. See Chapter 10 for descriptions of some cultivars and consult growers' catalogues for detailed descriptions.

Some of the 'Olds' will burst forth in a glorious fashion in the spring and not flower again until the following year, and others are repeat flowering; that is they flower again once the first flush of bloom is over, and keep this up throughout the year. Roses of this latter kind are also called 'remontant' and sometimes 'perpetual flowering'. The major families of Old-fashioned roses are as follows:

Species

This family comprises most of the earliest forms of the genus, many having single flowers. These wild roses grew originally in the Northern Hemisphere. Species roses are generally admired for simplicity of flower form and many are fragrant. If self-fertilised, they will breed true from seed.

Gallicas

Gallicas are usually of double form and the flowers open flat. The Gallica is noted historically as being the rose used for medicinal purposes. One of these, *R. gallica officinalis* is known still as the 'Apothecary's Rose' and the petals, when dried and powdered, retain their fragrance. It was this fragrance that was thought to be of benefit medicinally.

Damasks

These roses are usually strongly fragrant. The plants are of shapely growth and were grown in Ancient Persia, Rome and Greece, possibly being introduced to Europe by the Crusaders.

Albas

Albas were widely grown in the Middle Ages, possibly used medicinally. They tend to be large growers, and the flowers, while looking delicate in pale pastel, belie the tough and resilient nature of this group.

Centifolias

Centifolias are generally accepted as being brought to prominence by Dutch breeders in the seventeenth and eighteenth centuries. The flowers are big and globular in shape and have many petals. They are often referred to as 'Cabbage roses'.

Mosses

These roses are named for the moss-like growth on the stems and the buds and this moss can vary in appearance from one rose to another. Almost all of the Moss roses are highly fragrant, and they originated as 'sports', aberrations in growth, from a Centifolia in the eighteenth century. These are roses of great charm and unique beauty.

Portlands

Portlands were the first group of roses to reliably repeat flower. They have double flowers and many are fragrant.

Bourbons

Bourbons take their name from the Ile de Bourbon in the Indian Ocean, and which is now known as Reunion Islands. They are generally accepted as a hybrid, i.e., a cross between a Damask and a China rose. Bourbons generally repeat flower and are of compact growth habit. This group produces some of the most opulent of all roses.

Boursalts

This is a relatively small group, many having been lost to gardeners over time. They are generally thornless ramblers with long canes.

Chinas

With the introduction of this group, rose growing changed dramatically. China roses are reliably repeat flowering and of lighter growth habit than the earlier groups. The Chinas were introduced to Europe early in the eighteenth century and are rarely without blooms, which tend to be smaller than the blooms of earlier roses.

Noisettes

Noisettes require a warm growing position and some shelter to be at their best. Introduced in the early nineteenth century, this class includes some of the most beautiful climbing roses. Noisettes can be rampant growers and free flowering, and, as a bonus, most are fragrant.

Teas

The first Tea rose, 'Adam', was introduced into England in 1835. This name reflects the opinion that these roses had the fragrance of a chest of China tea. Tea roses generally have one profuse early flowering, with the ability to flower again later in the season. They tend to be of slender growth habit, with appealing soft colours.

Hybrid perpetuals

These roses are indeed hybrids, with possibly four of the above mentioned groups in their ancestry. They repeat flower and tend to have superb buds. Nearly all are fragrant and most will grow into large plants. There are no yellow roses in this class.

Rugosas

Rugosas are native to parts of Asia and they have a tendency to be very prickly plants. Many have single flowers which open flat to reveal prominent stamens. Almost all are very fragrant. Rugosas are vigorous plants and bear large, decorative heps (or hips) or seed pods. The leaves are rough and leathery looking, and these roses do extremely well in sandy, coastal conditions.

Hybrid musks

Hybrid musks are nearly always strongly fragrant and can be found in every possible colour and shade. They repeat flower and can be tall, strong growers. Their flowers tend to come in clusters and they are noted for their grace of growth habit and their ability to combine well visually with other plants in mixed beds.

Polyanthas

These roses are dwarf growers with double or semi double flowers. They are hardy, free flowering roses often displaying exquisite buds.

Ramblers

Ramblers generally flower only once in the season, but in great abundance. They are often rampant growers and rapidly cover fences and walls. Ramblers are also used as ground covers for large areas. Many are very fragrant and the flowers can vary from single to double. They have graceful, arching branches and can be trained to cover archways or scramble up trees. Some, like *Rosa wichuriana*, are of trailing habit and flexible growth and will drape themselves over banks.

Modern roses

Like the Old-fashioned roses, Modern roses come in different types, and within each type is a huge selection of cultivars from which to choose. Nearly all Modern roses are repeat flowering, and most can be purchased as Bush roses or as Standards.

Standard roses

Most roses are budded on to the stock of a very strong wild rose type (see Chapter 7). This gives the desired rose greater vigour. In most cases, the desired cultivar is budded on to a short rootstock, but in Standard roses the rootstock is left to grow much longer and the budding is done at about a metre above the ground. This creates, in effect, a rose 'tree'.

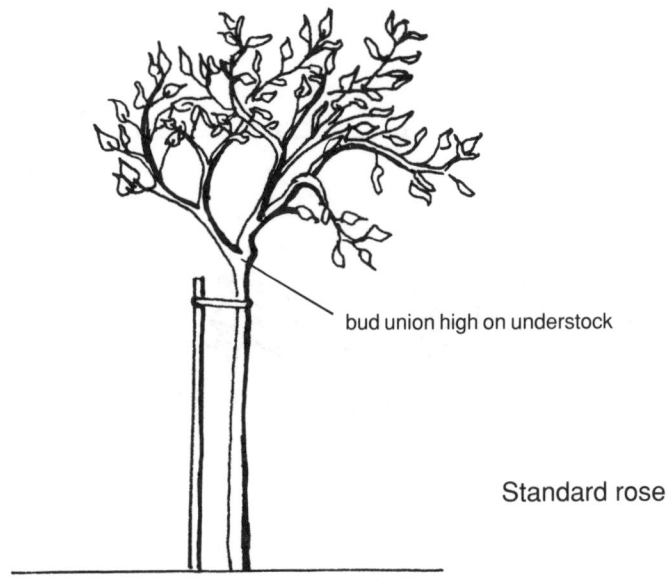

bud union high on understock

Standard rose

The term 'Standard' does not imply that a rose meets any defined quality or standard, it is simply a term used by rosarians to differentiate between these high budded plants and those on shorter understocks,

25

which are called 'Bush roses'. There is an enormous variety of cultivars which are routinely budded on as 'Standards' and some nurseries will even bud on Standards to order if your particular choice is not available in their catalogue. It is also possible to obtain miniature Standard roses and weeping Standard roses where the grower has budded a suitable cultivar on to the rootstock. So Standard roses are available in a very wide choice indeed, and the Standard is often the choice of those who wish to line a pathway or driveway leading to the house, or who want a more 'formal' look to their garden.

Standards require the same routine maintenance as Bush roses, but they do require rather more protection from strong winds than roses budded lower on the rootstock. If not well staked and tied in, Standards whip about in the wind and break off. In many cases, vigorous cultivars will grow as tall as standards even though budded on as Bush roses.

Bush roses

As mentioned above, most rose plants come under this heading and most are budded on to stronger rootstock. Many, however, are grown on their own roots from cuttings. There are advantages and disadvantages to both these methods of propagation, but it is the Bush rose that is most commonly grown in gardens today.

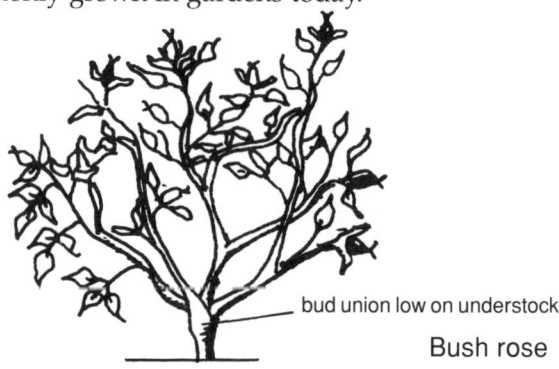

bud union low on understock

Bush rose

Types of modern roses

Hybrid teas/large flowered roses

Hybrid teas are available as Bush roses, Standards and sometimes as Climbers, depending on the cultivar. The name Hybrid tea refers to a class of roses that is a cross between Hybrid perpetuals and Tea roses.

Although Hybrid teas have been with us since the middle of the nineteenth century, they are still classed as Modern roses. The first of these Hybrid teas was possibly a rose named 'Victor Verdier', although 'La France' is usually acclaimed as the first of this new breed of rose. This category of rose is still the most popular type grown today, despite a resurgence of interest in the growing of Old-fashioned roses.

Hybrid teas continue to produce blooms from spring into winter in mild climates, and, in the warmer north, only pruning seems to prevent them from flowering throughout the year, albeit more slowly in the cooler months. Most Hybrid teas have large flowers, borne singly, and are unsurpassed as cut flowers. They are vigorous, hardy plants with long, pointed buds opening into high centred flowers, much admired by keen exhibitors.

With the Hybrid teas came an enormous interest in rose growing and a growth in the number of new roses being raised by hybridists. The Hybrid tea can be budded either high on the rootstock to produce a Standard or low to produce a Bush. Some Hybrid teas are available as Climbing roses, produced initially from a sport, and yet others are available *only* as climbers and have no bush form at all.

The Hybrid tea owes much of its popularity to its ability to flower repeatedly, and to the enormous range of flower colours and shapes available within the class ... a tribute to the many hybridists who have turned their attention to the Hybrid tea since its introduction over 120 years ago.

Floribundas/cluster flowered roses

These share the top favourite position with Hybrid teas at the present time and are sometimes called 'Cluster flowered roses'. Their distinguishing factor is their tendency to flower in large or small clusters as distinct from the Hybrid teas which mostly flower singly, and in this respect the Floribundas display their parentage as crosses between Hybrid teas and Polyanthas.

These roses are of vigorous habit, free flowering and have all the charcteristics of the Hybrid tea with regard to colour, fragrance and repeat flowering ability. Floribundas will create a mass of garden colour over a long period, and many Floribundas produce the high pointed flowers usually associated with Hybrid teas. Some of the newer cultivars are classified as Hybrid tea/Floribunda, indicating the closeness of the two classes and the blurring of the edges of classification between them.

Floribundas, like Hybrid teas, are generally budded on to rootstock and many cultivars have climbing forms. The flowers range from single, five-petalled flowers to very double and there will be a flower shape and colour to suit all tastes. Most floribundas are excellent as garden roses because of their ability to produce so many flowers on one shoot, and because of their reliable repeat flowering.

Climbing roses

This is not truly a class of its own as is indicated by the fact that many Hybrid teas and Floribundas can be obtained as Climbers. However, as distinct from the Ramblers which are rampant in growth, a Climber here is distinguished by the nature of its ancestry, i.e., it is usually a sport of a Hybrid tea or a Floribunda, or perhaps a Miniature.

Climbers are of inestimable value as garden plants, softening the outlines of buildings and fences and providing a background for other roses. They tend to have larger flowers and somewhat stiffer growth than Ramblers, and most Climbers are repeat flowering. They are more easily managed in a small garden situation than are Ramblers and a well grown Climber can be the most beautiful and abundant of all roses.

Miniature roses

Miniature roses are small-growing roses with flowers, foliage and other growth all in proportion. They are frequently grown on their own roots from cuttings, as many growers consider that budding tends to deprive the plants of their appealing smallness. Miniature rose plants can grow as small as 8 cm in height or as tall as 60 cm, and within the miniature range are roses with the characteristics of many of their larger relatives - Old-fashioned, Hybrid tea, Floribunda and climbing types - with flowers that can range from single to very double.

Many Miniatures are fragrant and all are suitable for tub or pot culture. Some climbing Miniatures can grow as large as 2 m, and ground cover Miniatures are also available. In the Southern Hemisphere, Miniatures tend to grow much larger than in Europe, and indeed this applies to most other roses, too. (Indications of size of plants given in books and catalogues of European origin cannot be relied upon as indicators of growth under our conditions.) For rose growers with small gardens, or even no garden at all, Miniatures are the answer to a prayer. They can be planted using just a kitchen spoon and pruning needs only the use of a sharp pair of scissors.

Patio roses

These are also small-growing roses and some growers prefer the term 'patio' to Miniature. Patio is sometimes used to describe the larger growing of the Miniature cultivars, and it is also sometimes used to describe Miniatures budded on to understock, in which case the plants grow larger than those grown on their own roots from cuttings.

English roses

It is difficult to place these roses in any of the foregoing classes, although many rosarians class them with the Floribundas. I prefer to put them in their own distinct class. Bred by David Austin of Shropshire, England, these roses were specifically raised to be Shrub rather than Bush roses. They were bred by crossing Old-fashioned roses with Modern roses, and Austin's aim was to combine 'the form, character and growth of the Old roses, with the repeat flowering habit and wider colour range of the Modern roses. English roses are, in fact, repeat flowering Old roses. '[1]

They have a more natural-looking, shrubby growth habit than the Hybrid teas and Floribundas and the flowers are of a shape more like the Old-fashioned roses, with all their colours leaning towards the pastel hues. David Austin aims to return delicacy to the rose and to capture 'that unique charm which we associate with Old roses.'[2] Nearly all of the English roses are strongly fragrant and are repeat flowering. Trevor Griffiths, a noted rose nurseryman and Old rose specialist said of the English roses in 1986, 'I have no doubt that these "new" old roses will be well received as they become better known and we must consider ourselves very fortunate to have access to them.'[3]

In the short years since that statement first appeared in print, Trevor Griffiths has been proved right. The English roses *are* better known now and are being planted all over the world by rose enthusiasts, and David Austin continues to hybridize and raise yet more 'new' Old roses.

From all of the above, it will be obvious that there is a kind of rose to fit every possible situation in the garden; pergolas, fences, mixed beds, cottage gardens, formal avenues, hedges. It only remains for the reader to select those kinds of roses that best suit, and in this selection process the gardener is well advised to consult the catalogues of reliable nurserymen. With such a wealth of superb roses to choose from, it is very difficult indeed to limit yourself once you've caught rose 'fever'!

4 Buying and planting

*Winter is the time when it is too cold to do the things
that it was too hot to do last summer.*

American Rose

There are two ways of buying rose plants. One is to purchase them as
'bare root' plants in winter, and the other is to purchase 'pot grown'
plants at any time of the year, with winter being the main planting time
for roses. Bare root plants, as the name suggests, are sold without soil,
and usually packaged in polythene. You may buy the plants from a local
garden centre, or you can order ahead of time from nurseries' catalogues. Most nurseries bud their plants on to rootstock, but some also
offer cutting grown plants, and the choice whether to bud or strike from
cuttings is made by the growers according to the difficulty of propagation or availability of propagating material. Some cultivars grow more
readily than others from cuttings, and others are only at their best when
budded on to strong rootstock. If you are buying via mail order from
catalogues, the grower will usually explain which roses are budded
and which are 'own root' plants. Plants in garden centres are usually
purchased in bulk from major nurseries.

Growers make every possible effort to present well grown, reliable
plants, and most will offer to replace any that fail to thrive when given
proper care. Garden centres will usually do this, too, so purchasing
roses either way is a pretty safe bet.

If you select some of the more unusual roses or Old roses, it is most
likely that these will only be available direct from the nurseries, as it is
not possible for garden centres to stock all available cultivars. In fact,
with some hard to propagate cultivars, the nursery may keep a 'when
available' listing and your order will be filled as and when these
cultivars are available in sufficient numbers to release. The reason for
this is that nurseries cannot possibly propagate every cultivar every
year, and so they have to use 'educated guesses' as to which ones to
propagate in any one year.

Many nurseries, in addition to offering bare root plants in winter, also offer pot grown plants throughout the year, or sometimes just in spring. Garden centres have their main selling period of bare root plants in winter, then tend to offer pot grown plants once they are in flower in the spring. So, the choice is yours, order from the mouth-watering descriptions of roses in growers' catalogues, or make your selection from what are usually the most popular cultivars at garden centres. It is as well to check that your choice of cultivar does well in your area.

If you choose to select your plant at a garden centre, look for one with at least two, and preferably three or four, strong canes growing from the budhead. Disregard the amount of top growth, as you will be cutting this off anyway at pruning time or a couple of weeks after the bush is planted. Most roses are *not* pruned before they are sent to garden centres; they are just cut back somewhat for ease of transportation.

Look also for bud 'eyes' that are looking plump, indicating that they will probably shoot later, as these will produce the flowering canes later in the season. Some plants will have begun to shoot already and the new growth will have a reddish tinge and be fresh looking and glossy. Damaged canes and foliage can be easily trimmed back, so don't be put off by those, just look for the strong canes at the budhead.

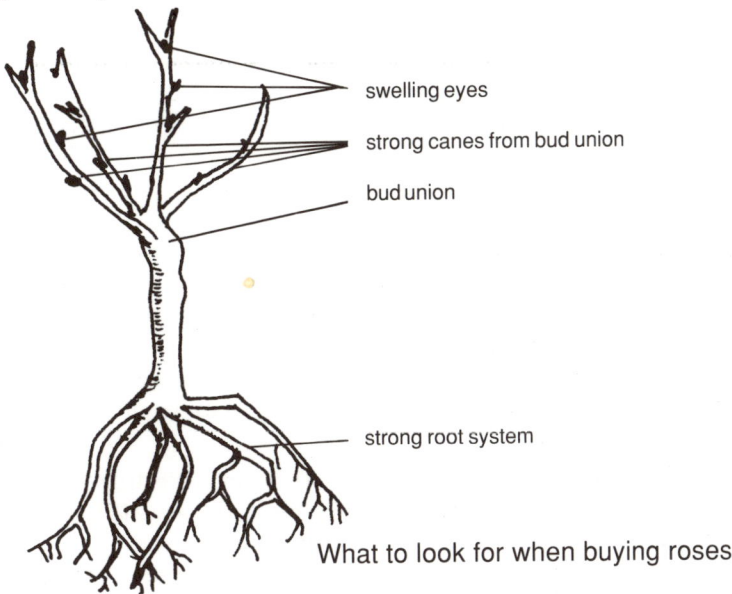

swelling eyes

strong canes from bud union

bud union

strong root system

What to look for when buying roses

You probably won't be able to see the roots as they will be enclosed in plastic and kept moist with shredded newspaper or wood shavings. Nurseries are very careful about packing their roses and this means keeping the roots in a moist condition. Packed like this, the plants will manage very well for many weeks in their bags, as long as the packing material is kept moist.

Roses are often available at supermarkets and chain stores as bare root plants. In most cases they will be very much cheaper than the same cultivars at garden centres or from nurseries. Many of these will grow and be perfectly satisfactory plants, but kept in the air-conditioned atmosphere of the supermarket for many weeks, the plants can deteriorate quite rapidly and lose moisture from their roots. In this situation they are unlikely to survive after you have planted them. Also, the temperature change from the enclosed supermarket to your garden is dramatic and such stress may cause the plants to die. So supermarket shopping for roses can be a very chancy business. It is more likely that you will gain satisfaction from plants purchased from the nurseries or from garden centres. Plants that appear on the face of it to be bargains are not always what they seem.

Planting bare root roses

Leave the plants in their protective packaging or put them into buckets of water with the roots submerged while you are getting their places ready. Rose roots exposed to sun or wind even briefly will dry out and, in any case, the plants can only benefit from a good, long 'drink' before planting. Leave them in the bucket until the last possible minute before putting them into the soil.

Mark out the places where the roses are to be planted. You will need to take into account the eventual size of your roses (across as well as up) to avoid having them too close together. Remember that they need air circulating around the foliage.

Have the name tags ready to insert in front of each plant *as it is planted;* it's amazing how fast you will forget which plant is which when you are planting even half a dozen roses. It's not a bad idea either to draw a plan of the bed with the name of each cultivar in its appointed place.

The hole you dig needs to be large enough to spread the roots out without bending or squashing them, so you will need to look at the size of the roots and the direction in which they are growing. Having done that, put the plant back into its water while you dig the hole.

Have a quantity of fine soil on hand as it will more readily settle around the roots. Planting mix is fine and often contains a slow-release fertiliser which will not burn the roots of new rose plants.

Make the hole deep enough so that the bud union will be just *above* the level of the soil when the hole is filled in. Some growers recommend placing the bud union below the soil surface to anchor the rose more firmly. Keeping it above the surface of the soil prevents unseen suckering from the rootstock and allows for later mulching. Deeper planting may be useful in extremely cold areas where frosts can damage the bud union, so in colder areas consider having the bud union below ground level. The danger with deeper planting is that suckers may well grow from below the bud union, sapping the strength from the budded cultivar. If the union is below the soil, you will have to dig around to find where the sucker begins in order to remove it at its source, and digging can damage the roots and produce more suckers. Either way, make sure that the roots of the rose are spread out and point *downwards*, as this will reduce the likelihood of sucker growth.

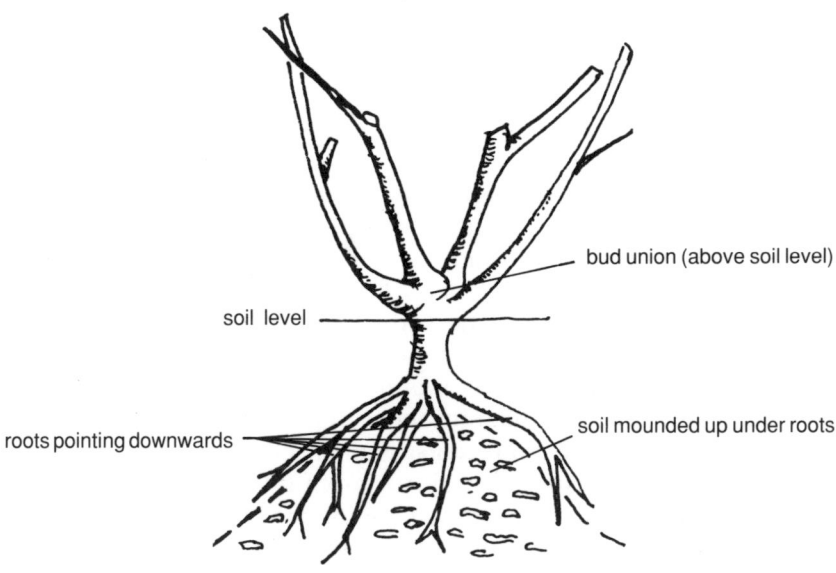

Planting

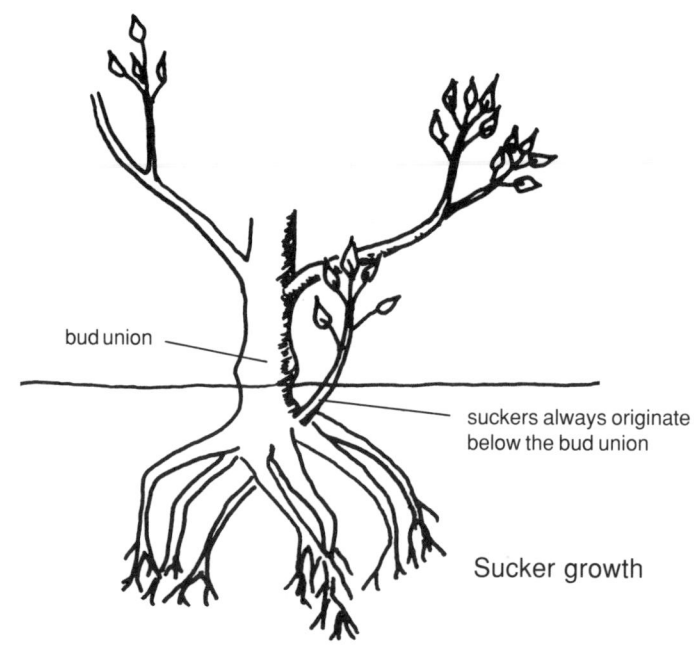

bud union

suckers always originate below the bud union

Sucker growth

The average spacing for various types of roses is as follows: Bush roses about 60 cm apart, varying this to allow for vigorous or small growers; Climbers need to be around 3 m apart, more if the cultivar is of vigorous habit; Standards can be spaced at any distance apart, but within the range of 1 to 2 m, depending on what you plan to do with the spaces in between the roses; and Miniatures should be spaced around 20 cm apart. Be guided by the advice in the catalogue or on the label as to the approximate size the plants will grow.

Having dug the hole and checked that its size is adequate for the roots, build a mound of fine soil in the centre of the hole. Hold the plant in position, sitting gently on this mound of soil so that the roots spread down and outwards (see diagram above). Fill in around the roots with more fine soil until the plant can support itself. Tread the soil down gently with your foot to settle it firmly around the roots.

Water in gently but thoroughly, allowing the hole to fill with water and then drain away. Then fill the hole with your good garden soil, treading in gently. Follow with another thorough watering. This will help the soil to settle properly around the roots and will eliminate any air pockets. You may, if you choose, add a little blood and bone in the soil at this stage, but *do not* add artificial fertilisers as these can burn the fine, new roots that will quickly grow now that the rose is in the ground.

Keep the soil moist but not soggy for a week or two after planting and your rose will be off to a flying start.

Planting Standard roses

This is done exactly as described above, but the bud union is of course around a metre, sometimes 2 m, above the roots, so in this case it will not influence the depth at which you plant. Aim to plant Standards at the same depth that they were planted at the nursery; you will be able to gauge this from the mark on the rootstock.

With Standards, a stake must *always* be used to support each plant, so after digging the hole, drive the stake in firmly *before* you continue with the actual planting. A stake driven in after planting can do irreparable damage to the roots of the rose. Wooden stakes are adequate, and each rose must be tied to its stake with just one tie at the top of the plant, preferably with the tie threaded through the canes. If a tie is applied lower down the rootstock, a strong wind can cause the rootstock to bend and even break off at the point where the tie is made, so make it just one tie and make it firm.

You may choose to stake your Bush roses initially, too, especially if planting in an open area. If you do this, drive the stake in *before* planting the rose and tie in firmly. Garden string is the best tying material. Wire may cut into the canes and damage them, especially if ties are not checked regularly.

Climbing roses

Climbing roses are planted in the same way as Bush and Standard types, but do allow about 30 cm between the plant and the support on which it will grow. This makes for easier weeding later. If the rose is planted too close to its support you may find yourself lying on the ground trying futilely to grasp at weeds without tearing your hands and arms to pieces on low-growing canes!

Your newly planted roses will be ready to be pruned back about three weeks after planting and this will give them every chance to grow and flourish.

Planting pot grown roses

Throughout the year, at garden centres and sometimes direct from nurseries, pot grown roses can be purchased. These are usually grown in black polythene planter bags and are grown in a potting mix. Roses grown in this way can be planted out at any time of the year, but avoid very hot, dry periods. Give the potted plant a very thorough soaking the day (or at least a few hours) before you plant, to ensure that the roots are well moistened. Dig the hole as for bare root plants, then cut the plastic from around the rose. Don't just pull the plant from the bag.

Some roses grown in pots will have become 'pot bound'; that is they have been in the bag too long and their roots, in trying to find somewhere to grow, have gone round and round inside the pot, making a tangled mess which can be very difficult to sort out without injury to the root system. Lie the plant on its side and try tapping at the root system to see if some of the potting mix will fall away. If tapping doesn't produce the desired result, try using a hand fork or tread gently on the root mass to loosen the soil. You can also use a jet of water from a hose to remove the mix from the roots.

The nutrients in the potting mix will have been used up and it is best to discard most of it when planting the rose out. Even if you succeed in removing part of the mix, that will help. Long and very tangled root systems may be trimmed off with secateurs for ease of planting.

Make sure that all the roots are pointing downwards and settle the plant into the hole, filling in around it with planting mix or good garden soil, watering it in and treading it gently down as for bare root plants. Have the surface soil at the same level as the rose was planted in the pot; you will see the mark on the rootstock. Allow, as in planting bare root roses, for deeper planting in hard frost areas.

Heeling in

Sometimes it is not possible to plant your new roses as soon as you would like, for instance if the garden soil is extremely wet and muddy and impossible to dig. In such cases, it is vitally important to arrange for temporary quarters for the new plants. This is known as 'heeling in'. Dig a shallow trench in any suitable part of the garden and lie the plants in it along one side and a few centimetres apart. The plants should be laid at an angle of about 45 degrees.

Cover the roots well with soil and water in heavily. Heeled in like this, your roses will remain in good condition until you are ready to plant them, even if they have to remain like this for months. Do remember, however, to keep the labels out of the soil and still attached to each individual plant.

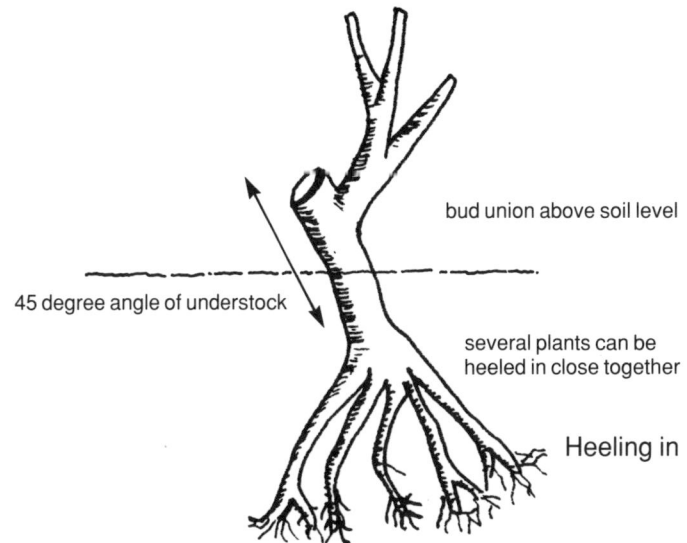

bud union above soil level

45 degree angle of understock

several plants can be
heeled in close together

Heeling in

Replacing roses

In established gardens, many rose plants are bought to replace older ones or plants that have proved unsatisfactory in one way or another. When this is the case, it is usual to dig out the plant to be replaced in autumn if this is possible. When digging it out, remove the soil in which it is growing along with the plant's root system, which in older plants may be quite considerable. Dig out further soil from the hole; around a barrow-load is ideal. This soil is *not* suitable for new roses and is termed 'rose sick'.

There is a divergence of opinion on just what causes this condition. Two possibilities usually suggested are depletion of nutrients or that the rose's roots give off toxins which cause a bacterial imbalance in the soil, preventing essential nutrients getting to the new rose in adequate quantities. Whatever the reason, new roses will not grow in soil where other roses have been, so you need to replace the old soil with new. Plant the rose in the new soil according to whether it is bare root or pot grown. You may safely use the discarded soil in another part of the garden.

Roses should *not* be planted when the soil is unworkable from heavy rain, during a hot, dry spell, or during the hottest part of the day. In summer, plant in the evening or during a cloudy or rainy spell. If planting pot grown roses in summer, do keep the soil moist for a few weeks after planting and apply a thick mulch. The mulch helps to lessen evaporation and gives the roses a cool root run. Roses are generally deep rooting plants, but they need protection from the hot sun until they establish their root systems deep in the soil.

5 Pests and diseases

Out came my little spray again,
First picking off with care
All damaged leaves - I must admit
This left some bushes bare!

Lettie Cole

In comparison with the beauty that roses will bring, the pest and disease department is very small indeed. If you plant in suitable sites and feed appropriately, diseases need not be a problem. In roses, as with animals (including humans), the better fed and healthier they are, the less likely they are to be troubled by disease. Certainly there are some pests that will attack roses, but no more than will attack any other garden plant. Good hygiene will prevent many diseases, and most pests can be easily dealt with. Also, plants are unlikely to die because of pests or diseases.

Systemic pesticides and fungicides are commonly available and will offer protection from most of the common diseases and pests. These systemic products are absorbed by the plant via its foliage and are then carried to all other parts of the plant. Systemic products are usually in concentrated form and are diluted with water before use. You can use the same sprayer as is used for foliar feeding, and often the fungicides and pesticides can be combined with the foliar feed to do three jobs at once. Be guided by the printed directions, however, and if in doubt ask a nurseryman or contact the manufacturers.

With sprays, don't assume that if 5 ml per litre is good, then 10 ml will be better. This is simply not the case, and you could end up damaging the foliage. Keep your rose sprayer just for the roses and *never* use it to apply weedkiller. It's just too easy to forget about some residue that may be left, and weedkiller is a herbicide that will kill roses too.

Pests

Aphids

Aphids are the tiny green insects that mass themselves on new rose growth, covering small buds and new leaves with a mossy green carpet. They suck the sap from the plant and can cause sooty mould, a blackish fungus that grows on the honey dew secreted by the aphids.

Aphids can be sprayed with a contact insecticide of course, but they can also be squashed easily between your finger and thumb. As they reproduce at an astonishing speed, you will have to keep up your preferred aphid control method every few days, at least in spring, and possibly throughout the growing season. Many people swear by an application of soapy water from dish washing or clothes washing, and this will certainly remove the insects, as will a good squirt from a hose.

Systemic insecticides usually containing maldison are absorbed by the foliage and make the sap toxic for some weeks. This makes them an extremely effective method of aphid control. Read the directions on the container carefully, and check to see if the product is safe to use where there are bees and birds.

Snails and slugs

These garden pests are not usually a menace to roses, but rose seedlings need to be protected so that they aren't decimated by the odd snail or slug on his way to the lettuces. Snail and slug baits are available and easy to use. Some are extremely toxic, however, not only to pests, but also to soil bacteria and earthworms.

Caterpillars

Caterpillars aren't usually a big problem and succumb readily to the finger and thumb method, or you can squash them underfoot after picking them off the undersides of leaves. If preferred, you can spray plants with a product formulated for killing chewing insects; such products often contain maldison.

Thrips, mites and red spider mites

These can all be troublesome in some areas and thrips can cause major damage in spring. They are tiny black winged insects and cause most of their damage by getting into rose buds, which will then fail to open.

Thrips seem to appear mainly in dry, inland areas. A carbaryl-based spray will kill them.

Red spider mites, too, are worse in dry weather. They lurk on the undersides of leaves, and are the main suspects if leaves drop prematurely or if the leaves have a yellow/red tinge. Closer inspection will reveal that the patch of colour is actually a moving mass of mites.

Like aphids, thrips and red spider mites reproduce at an astonishing speed, so prompt action is needed. Miticides are available to spray on the foliage if the infestation is very bad, but generally a good, strong spray with the hose every few days will solve the problem. Concentrate the spray on the undersides of the leaves.

Scale insect

Areas of white spots on sheltered parts of the plants are scale insects, which are sap suckers and often appear in late summer and autumn. Warm areas may also have scale in spring, and, if unchecked, this can cause harm to the plants. This is one case where the hose will *not* do the trick, as the scales of the insects are waterproof. An oil spray in winter is a good 'clean up' for any lingering insects, especially if you add maldison to the oil for a good kill. It may be necessary to spray again (usually at a diluted rate) if scale is seen in spring. There are also specific insecticides for scale.

Diseases

With good plant siting and feeding, your problems with disease will be minimal, and rose breeders all over the world are working to breed disease-resistant cultivars. Rose trial grounds world-wide are operating and assessing new cultivars for disease resistance as well as general garden performance, so particularly susceptible cultivars are less likely to win awards from trial grounds. Trial Ground Certificates greatly enhance the prospects of specific cultivars being commercially successful. There are, however, just a few persistent diseases that commonly occur in roses.

Black spot

If unchecked, this disease can quickly defoliate rose plants. It is so named because black/brown spots appear on the leaves usually circled with yellow. Leaves so affected will drop, thus lessening the plant's ability to absorb elements needed for food from the atmosphere.

A badly affected plant may need to be cut back. Burn all of the fallen and infected cuttings and leaves, as spores from this fungus disease are carried by contact and by the wind. It is not possible to cure the disease, so prevention is the way to go. Fungicide sprays are available and are often already mixed with insecticides to reduce the amount of work needed in the garden. Reduction of soil temperature by mulching and keeping the plants growing strongly will help them to resist this disease.

Rust

This is another fungus disease that may affect roses, and one which can be difficult to eradicate or control. Rust is not as widespread as black spot, but it, too, can cause defoliation. Rust appears as tiny orange spots on the undersides of leaves; as its name suggests. Cut back badly affected plants and burn the cuttings.

Rust seems to appear only in some years, and then it is not seen again for several years. However, it can spread very rapidly and after trimming back badly affected plants, spray with fungicide. Preventive spraying is a better option for fungus diseases. Note that some rose cultivars are more susceptible to rust than others. Sprays containing copper as cupric hydroxide are the most effective in preventing this and other fungus diseases.

Mildew

There are two types of mildew that commonly attack roses. Powdery mildew is the most commonly seen. It is often noticed in spring or autumn, usually appearing where air circulation is inadequate. Large differences between night and day temperatures seem to favour its growth. Leaves, stems and buds show greyish white powdery surfaces.

Remove any affected parts from the plant, as there will be no flowers on parts so affected and the disease will spread if unchecked. Appropriate sprays will protect against the disease and affected plants can be cured by trimming and spraying.

Powdery mildew is practically waterproof and a suggested form of treatment is to spray with your selected product as directed with the addition of a spreader or sticker. Then hose off the spray after two hours. Spray again, this time leaving the spray on the foliage.

Downy mildew consists of purplish brown blotches on the leaves and it can defoliate a plant. The disease can spread and prevent buds from opening. Spring seems to be the main season for this disease, which, like powdery mildew, can be controlled by trimming and spraying with a copper-based product.

Lime sulphur spray should be applied in early winter to kill the spores of most diseases which can live through the winter on dead leaves on the surface of the soil. This should then be followed by a copper and horticultural oil spray three weeks later. This programme will eradicate left over spores from the previous season and so prevent outbreaks of disease later when the plants are beginning to grow strongly.

Proprietary sprays

Always use proprietary sprays in accordance with instructions on the label. If one type of spray appears to be losing its effect, change to one with a different active ingredient. If in doubt, consult a nurseryman or local rose society. Powder sprays can be mixed with a little milk or oil to help the spray to stick to the foliage. A commercial spreader/sticker is another option.

There are many insecticides and fungicides available and most can be found in garden centres and often in supermarkets, too. If you prefer a powder to a spray, these are available for sprinkling on the foliage. Most products are multiple use and this can be very convenient for gardeners with limited time.

Use all sprays carefully. Wear protective clothing and spray only on still days. Wash any exposed skin thoroughly after spraying and store sprays in their original containers well out of the reach of children.

Petal fleck virus

There is another, more insidious disease of roses, and this is Petal Fleck Virus. This virus disease can be on the understock or on the scion (the budded cultivar), or both. There is no way that a buyer can know of the virus's presence when purchasing a plant and there is no cure. Affected plants must be destroyed by burning.

The presence of the virus may often only be distinguished by the symptoms that the flowers show. In red roses, in particular, the petals will show fine lines running towards the edge of the petals, as though applied by a paint brush. The virus is less noticeable in paler reds and oranges, and may escape notice entirely in pale yellow, cream or white roses. The fine lines have a vein-like appearance and are usually of a darker colour than the rest of the petal. It is often only possible to detect this virus by comparing a flower from the affected plant with one from a 'clean' plant.

Plants bought from a source that advertises 'High Health' roses *should* be free of viruses, and if you find that a High Health rose has this virus, you have every right to make a very large fuss indeed and return the plant. Plants with the virus are generally poorer all over with less flowers and premature dying back of canes, and the leaves have flecks or yellow lines. Rose nurseries are all aware of the problems associated with this virus and most are attempting to present stock that is virus free and truly 'high health'.

'Green' rose growing

It is possible to prevent major outbreaks of disease by good garden hygiene. The dangers of misuse of chemicals in horticulture is too well documented to require elaboration here. Never spray insecticides for prevention only, and when you feel that you *must* spray, do so selectively; only where the insects are in evidence.

Be aware that many insecticides also kill bees, ladybirds and praying mantises as well as aphids. Insecticides, like many chemicals are a two-edged sword. Natural predators like ladybirds and praying mantises will gobble up lots of aphids if you give them the chance to do so. Transfer any praying mantises you see on to the roses and leave them to get the aphids for you. Many small birds love aphids, too, and should be encouraged in your garden. A well-planned patch of native plants will help to keep the birds in and around your garden.

Soapy water is a good removal method for aphids, but do remember to repeat it every few days as their breeding rate is phenomenal! Many common garden plants will also act as deterrents to insects, and can be planted among the roses (see Chapter 11).

A measure you can take to avoid the over-use of fungicides is to select cultivars that are noted for their disease resistance. *Always* collect and burn all fallen leaves, as well as any diseased parts of plants that you trim off at any time of the year. Never put this potentially harmful material in the compost heap, as the fungus spores will multiply there ready to attack the roses again next year when you use the compost.

Keep the plants growing strongly with plenty of organic food. Inorganic fertilisers may have harmful effects on earthworms and soil bacteria, causing the soil to be depleted of micro-organisms and to need yet more fertilisers. If you are unable to make your own compost or use blood and bone to feed the roses, ask at your garden centre for an organic rose food.

The major manufacturers of garden products are fully aware that we all want to practise ecologically sound gardening, and some have come up with their own ranges of safer products often based on pyrethrum or fatty acids (potassium salts). Look for these at garden centres, and be sure to read the labels thoroughly so that you know exactly what is in the product and what effect it will have. For mite control, biological predators are available commercially; these are often advertised in gardening magazines.

6 Pruning

There is no rose bush whatsoever but prospereth the better
for cutting, pruning, yea and burning.

Pliny (AD 23-74)

There is no aspect of rose growing so feared by the beginner as pruning. Perhaps people feel threatened by pruning 'experts' who predict dire and terrible consequences for roses that are not pruned according to their rules. This is all absolute nonsense! There are as many ways of pruning as there are people who grow roses, and whatever you do or don't do in the way of pruning, you will still have roses in the season. Pruning is not an exact science or a military operation to be carried out with serious frowns or rulers. It helps the plants to produce more blooms and it conserves the plant's strength so that it is not wasted on unproductive growth. It also keeps the plant conforming to a desired shape.

You cannot kill a rose by pruning it, there is no wrong way to prune, and it is an ideal excuse to spend more time in the garden. If you wish, you can put on a very dedicated, serious face, take a pair of secateurs in your hand and march solemnly out to the garden 'to prune my roses'. Nobody will disturb you for hours! Incidentally, if you don't prune your roses, you'll still get flowers, albeit rather less each year. To prove this to yourself, look at the roses growing wild in the countryside, which still bloom after years of not being pruned.

Basically, we prune roses to maintain their health. It really is as simple as that. By cutting out old, unproductive wood we allow the plant to throw out new, vigorous stems which will flower for some years. Left unpruned, a rose will quickly become very crowded with twiggy growth. This growth diverts nutrients that would otherwise be used for the production of new canes and flowers. Clearing the centre of the rose of old wood also allows light and air into the bud union and allows you to remove any material that may harbour diseases.

45

The major pruning of roses is done in winter. This is because plants are then in their most dormant state. In most of the Southern Hemisphere, roses will flower for longer than in the colder climates of England and much of North America, and pruning in our milder climates does not need to be as hard. Late pruning in cold climates is practised because after pruning the new growth encouraged will come away quite quickly and may be damaged by heavy frosts. In addition, cold-climate gardeners may need to protect plants from the extreme cold by hilling up soil, leaves or other protective material around the base of each plant until the warmer weather of spring.

Most rose growers in the Southern Hemisphere will prune around mid to late July, earlier in warm districts and later in areas where frosts occur. Your roses will not bloom earlier in the spring just because you prune them earlier; the only way to have early blooms is to plant early flowering cultivars.

Tools for pruning

The equipment necessary for pruning includes some strong gloves. For rose pruning, it is best that the gloves have leather on the backs of the hands, as this is where most scratches will occur. The fingers need to be leather too, as the rose thorns will stab straight through fabric gloves. Next, you need good, sharp secateurs; buy the best you can afford and look after them well. They will last many years. Don't use your rose secateurs for other work, particularly heavy shrub and tree pruning, as this may damage them and will certainly blunt the blades. Hold the secateurs so that the cutting blade is underneath, nearest to the bush. This way the wood being retained will not be crushed or squeezed. Any damage to the wood being removed will not matter.

If you have large growing roses, a pruning saw or a lopper may be needed for thick branches that cannot be cut with secateurs. A lopper is much like a pair of secateurs, but you can apply greater force as the tool has long handles. Do wear protective clothing, especially for your arms, and solid soled shoes. Stepping on a large thorn in bare feet can be a very unpleasant business! A sheet or large bin that you can drag about the garden with you and drop the prunings into as you go will save having to pick up all the rubbish later.

When you use a saw or lopper to cut out thick branches, it is as well to protect the newly made cut with pruning paste to prevent the entry of disease. Make sure that the product you use is one that is specially formulated for roses. A product designed for fruit trees can result in severe dieback. A copper and oil spray immediately after pruning will also seal the pruning cuts. You can, if you choose, disinfect your secateurs after pruning each plant to prevent the carry over of disease from one plant to another. Many growers advise this precaution.

Hybrid teas

These roses can be pruned light, medium or hard, according to the growth habit of each plant, the size you want the bush to be and your own inclination. There is no lack of theories about how hard to prune. Many of the advocates of heavy pruning have adopted this practice from British techniques, which are designed for quite a different climate. How hard to prune your roses is *your* decision.

Have a good look at the bush before you start and see which canes are strong and young; these will be greenish brown or perhaps reddish in colour. Old canes tend to be greyish and will as a rule be thick and woody. Also, look to see if any parts of the bush are of the '3D' variety; that is dead, diseased or deformed. Take a deep breath and cut out *all* of this 3D growth right back flush to the bud union.

Next, remove any branches which have grown across the centre of the bush. When the new growth starts in spring, crowding in the centre will prevent air circulation and sunlight reaching the bud union. If left, these branches will also rub against each other and the foliage may be damaged.

If a new basal shoot is appearing from the bud union, try to make room for it or else gently encourage it to head off to the side by tying it. These new basal shoots are very tender, so treat them gently. You should now be left with a somewhat vase-shaped bush, with only strong canes growing up and outwards. If your plants don't seem to conform to this description and have all of the good canes growing on one side, just accept that and proceed anyway.

If you have lots of good canes, then you can afford to cut out the older ones right back to the bud union. The older canes will be browner and have vertical lines on them. When cutting them out, take care not to leave little stumpy bits that will collect and hold debris around the bud union. Plan to keep as many big basal shoots as you can as this is the framework for your bush in future years. Now cut out the thinnest of any branches that will cross others, possibly causing damage later. As older branches will produce less flowers, when you need to make a choice between cutting out an old cane and a young one, cut out the old one. Keep the bush as young as possible as older plants will produce less basal shoots.

Now shorten the remaining canes, retaining the ones that seem to be best placed. Most canes will have lots of little branches and growth at the top and all of this needs to be removed. Then cut back all canes to about half of their current height and remove any twiggy growth that is still about. When you make these shortening cuts, try with each cut you make to cut just *above* a bud facing in the direction that you want the new shoot to grow. Usually you will want the new shoot to grow outwards, but it may suit your purpose to prune to an inwards facing bud. The main issue here is that you prune to a *live* bud; one that will shoot from the eye, and sometimes there just isn't an outward facing bud in the right place, so cut to the nearest suitable *live* bud.

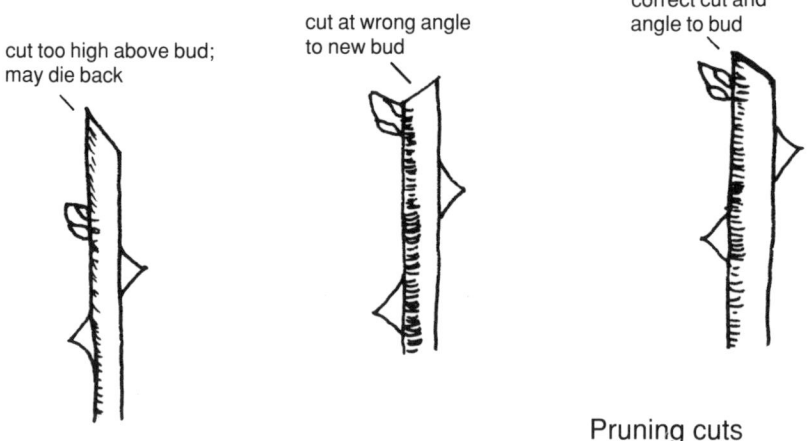

cut too high above bud; may die back

cut at wrong angle to new bud

correct cut and angle to bud

Pruning cuts

Light pruning will leave your bushes larger, so more blooms will come, but possibly these will be smaller in comparison with those on a harder pruned bush. Roses that are pruned *very* hard sometimes develop a sluggish root system, and this can cause the whole plant to lose vitality. On the other hand, fairly hard pruning of a spindly, weak grower may help to increase its growth. You will find advocates of both sorts of pruning, but ultimately you will make your own decisions. Remember that however you prune, it can never be 'wrong' and you will learn more every year by watching your roses grow.

Basal shoots, or water shoots as they are sometimes called, which grow from the bud union, are pruned in a different way from the rest of the bush. In very cold areas they are cut right back because late frosts will kill them anyway, but in milder areas these shoots are precious because of their potential to be flowering canes in later years. They will usually be topped by little groups of buds on very short stems and it is only this top growth that is removed in the first winter's pruning. By the next winter, the wood will have matured and can be pruned in the usual way with the rest of the bush. When you have finished pruning the bush, you may end up with branches of varying length. This is perfectly acceptable, but if the shape annoys you, you can even it up a bit, cutting, as before, just above a live bud.

Floribundas

Floribundas can be pruned as above, cutting out all 3D canes, thus encouraging basal shoots and making sure that the centre of the bush is kept clear.

Standard roses

Prune as above, but usually a little harder to balance the heavy top growth with the fine, tall stem. Renew ties on Standards after pruning each year.

Miniature roses

These are also pruned in the manner described above, but the only tool that a Miniature rose grower will need is a sharp pair of scissors, with possibly secateurs for older canes and larger-growing cultivars.

Climbing roses of the Hybrid tea or Floribunda type

The same basic principles apply to climbing roses when pruning. Cut out all 3D wood to keep the plant young, and shorten the canes that you intend to keep. It is as well to remove all the ties before you begin to prune Climbers.

The long canes should be trained horizontally in a fan shape, with the newest canes at the top and centre of the fan, older canes being gradually lowered towards the bottom each year as new ones shoot from the bud union. Do not bend the canes down further than the horizontal. Cut out the oldest, lower canes at pruning time and lower the others, tying in each cane as you go. Shorten the remaining canes to three or four growth 'eyes', pruning, as before, to a live bud.

I have heard it said that pruning newly planted Climbers will result in the plant somehow reverting to a Bush rose. This really is utter nonsense as the Climber is genetically different from the Bush and it just isn't possible to alter genetic codes by surgery. When George Washington cut down the fabled Cherry Tree, he didn't create a Cherry *Bush*; all he did was to make a very short tree! Climbers cut back hard will certainly take longer to grow long canes again, but they will always be Climbers.

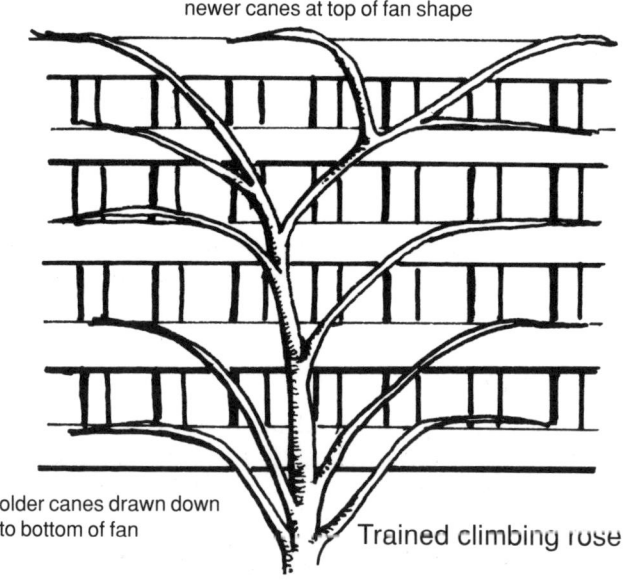

newer canes at top of fan shape

older canes drawn down
to bottom of fan

Trained climbing rose

Rambling roses of the Old-fashioned type

Most of these, unlike the previously described roses, flower on wood grown the previous year. It is just as important, however, to remove 3D wood and the oldest canes and to protect new growth shooting from the bud union. Around April you can remove all the old canes that have flowered as they will not flower again. Tie in new canes firmly to protect them from wind damage. If new growths have not come from the bud union in some years, old canes may need to be retained, but in such cases cut them back harder. Ramblers can become a tangled mess very quickly, so don't let them get away on you. Trying to make sense of a tangled old Rambler can be very difficult if it has been allowed to remain unpruned for some years.

Old-fashioned roses

In general, all that is necessary is to remove the 3D growth, and much will depend on whether the particular cultivar is repeat flowering or not. A rose society will help here, as will rose nurseries. Most Old roses bloom on mature wood and so must not be cut back as hard as the more modern cultivars or you will find yourself without flowers. Some, on the other hand, are 'ever blooming' and will even bloom in winter, so it is as well to seek detailed advice from specialists.

Suckers

These are shoots from the understock of the plant; the part on to which your rose has been budded. Suckers must be removed at their *source* or they will grow vigorously at the expense of the 'scion', the budded cultivar. This is a very good reason for keeping the bud union above soil level when planting. A sucker, if just cut back, will grow with even greater vigour, so it is vital to remove it at its point of origin below the bud union.

The sucker may originate from the roots or from the stem of the understock via an eye that has not been cut out and suckers are recognised by having thinner stems than those of basal shoots. The foliage on a sucker is usually smaller than that of the scion, and it will not have buds at its tip. Even if the process involves some digging, this growth must be removed at its point of origin. Cut through the part of the root where the sucker originates and remove it, being sure to leave all the other roots pointing down into the soil. If the sucker originates from the stem of the understock, you can slice it out with a sharp knife.

It is not generally wise to dig about in rose beds as roots may be damaged and small pieces of root left upturned can produce further sucker growth. Try not to have plants that require digging up, like dahlias, in your rose beds. To remove weeds, use a shallow hoe or cultivator. Any trampling about in any sort of rose beds is to be avoided too, as this can compact the soil, preventing the escape of gases and the aeration of the roots.

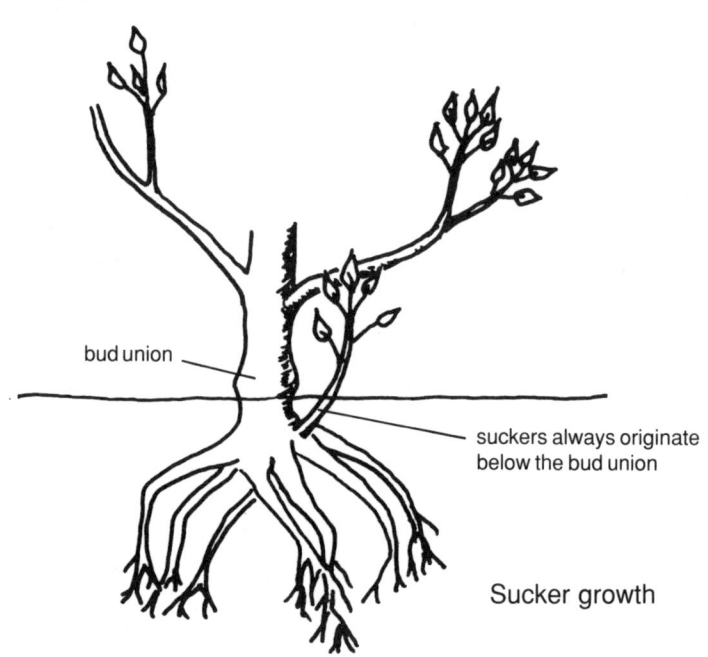

bud union

suckers always originate below the bud union

Sucker growth

Summer trimming for autumn blooms

Unlike spring flowering, which is determined by climatic factors and by cultivar tendency, autumn flowering can be timed with reasonable accuracy by trimming, feeding and watering at appropriate times. If you prefer to leave your roses to bloom as they choose, you will have a good spring flush of blooms and then another about six weeks later, if you remember to dead-head the flowers as they fade. After that, there will not be as many blooms in most areas as rainfall is generally lower and further growth and flowering is retarded by this factor. By April, less blooms appear, gradually decreasing in number and quality, though occasional cultivars will continue to produce blooms until pruned back.

By trial and error, we are able to encourage a much bigger and better flush of blooms in autumn by 'summer trimming' repeat flowering roses in February. Although the timing of the 'summer trim' will vary according to different climates, the process remains the same.

From about Christmas, rose beds should not be watered, except in abnormally dry conditions where just a little extra water can be given to help the plants to survive the hot weather. Also, faded blooms should be cut off with only the heads being removed at this time of year. Flowers for display indoors should be cut with only short stems. This will tend to encourage new growth to come high on the stems and the stems will mature.

Then in early February, water very heavily indeed, adding your watering to any rain that falls. Feed the roses lightly, then water well again to further stimulate the high growth on the stems. The plants are being pushed into rapid growth at this stage. A week later, it is time for the trimming, which is different from the winter pruning. Go over each bush, cutting stems exactly as if you were cutting long stemmed roses for the house. Keep the soil moist now and give another feeding after a further two weeks, again watering in well and continuing to keep the beds moist to keep the plants growing well.

Do keep up with the spray programme while all this work is going on, as pests and diseases will flourish in the strong new growth that is appearing. Growth will be extremely fast for a few weeks, gradually slowing as cooler nights approach, and it is vital to keep watering, giving a particularly heavy soaking in late March or early April. You will be rewarded for your efforts by a splendid flush of bloom later in April and May that will far surpass the spring blooming.

Generally speaking, the peak of the autumn blooming will occur around seven weeks after the trimming, but you may need to make some adjustment according to your district. If you trim later than very early February, cooler soil temperatures will delay the peak flowering till possibly nine or ten weeks from the trimming date. Leave very new basal shoots out of the 'summer trim' as the process may well kill them. More mature basals can have just their tips trimmed.

There will be lots more blooms in autumn as the plants will be bigger than in spring and many rose societies hold autumn shows. A year or two of practice with the 'summer trim' will make you more able to time it with precision and the roses will look their best at a time of *your* choosing.

7 Propagation

*Ere one flowery season fades and dies
Design the blooming wonders of the next.*

Anon

Roses can be propagated by three methods. The first is by cuttings, layering or tissue culture and is essentially propagation by cloning. That is, the creation of a new plant from cells of the same genetic constitution as the parent plant. These are called 'own root' plants.

The second method of propagation is by tying in a bud of the wanted cultivar on to a rootstock of another rose, usually a stronger growing and rooting one, often *Rosa multiflora*. These budded roses comprise the majority of nursery grown plants and are called 'budded roses'.

The third method is by sexual reproduction, i.e., seeds. The rose is a hermaphrodite; that is it contains both male and female parts and is capable of self-fertilisation, producing seeds which are contained in the heps (or hips) which ripen after the flowers have faded. In this case, because of the complex ancestry of roses, the seed grown plants will be different from the parents, whether minimally or markedly, and also different from each other. This is how new roses are produced, by selecting the parents according to the characteristics wanted in the new cultivar The pollen of one flower is used to fertilise another.

Cuttings

This is the easiest of all propagation methods, and the one that can be employed most readily by gardeners who are keen to increase their collections of roses. There are admittedly some cultivars that are difficult to 'strike' as cuttings, but most will put down roots relatively quickly. Cuttings of roses can be taken from summer until pruning time in winter, with the optimum time being around April.

Select a strong straight piece off the current year's growth, preferably from a cane that has flowered. About 20 cm is a good length for most cultivars, but miniatures need only be about 8 cm long. The cutting does not need to have a heel of old wood on it. Cut off all the leaves and ensure that the cutting has several growth eyes in its upper half. Make a horizontal cut at the bottom just *below* a good eye. Make the top cut *above* an eye, and slant it up towards the eye; this will also enable you to tell the tops of cuttings from the bottoms if you are making a number of them.

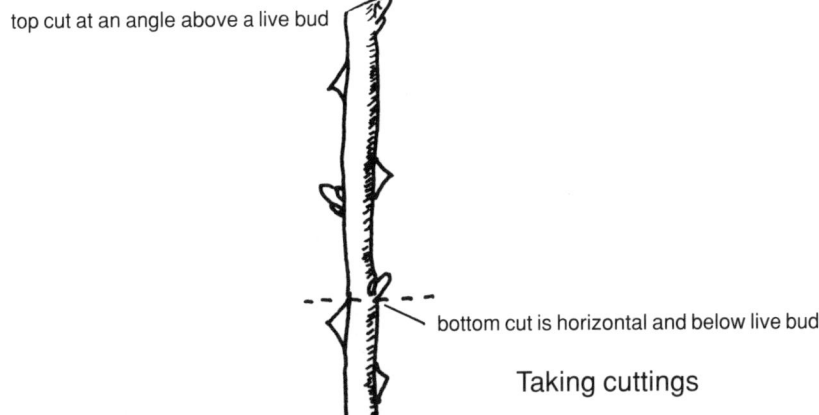

top cut at an angle above a live bud

bottom cut is horizontal and below live bud

Taking cuttings

Keep the cuttings moist, preferably in a deep container of water, until you are ready to plant them. A good, long drink, even for a day or two, will not harm the cuttings and will ensure that they are turgid when they are planted. Some people like to put a little honey in the water, claiming a better strike rate this way. Perhaps you could try some soaked in the honey water and some not, then plant in separate pots and see for yourself. If you choose, you may also like to dip the end to be planted in hormone powder to encourage root formation, but this is by no means essential.

The best medium for striking cuttings is a sandy, free draining one; use fine river gravel, horticultural pumice, vermiculite or perlite, all commonly available at garden centres. Otherwise, fine, sandy garden soil will do. Insert the cuttings deep into the medium in deep pots to allow root growth, or, if you prefer, plant them directly into a trench in the garden which has been filled with the cutting medium. Some growers add peat to their cutting medium, but others prefer straight pumice.

If you are making a number of cuttings, they can be inserted very close together without any ill effects, but make sure to label them as you go. Insert the cuttings with two-thirds of their length in the medium and firm them down very well, then water in thoroughly so that the medium compacts down and settles firmly against the base of the cuttings. Keep the medium moist and do not disturb the cuttings for about two months. Many cuttings will strike within a couple of weeks, but the new roots that grow so quickly will not be strong, so leave them be, just ensuring an adequate supply of moisture at all times.

The cuttings may often show top growth quite early, tricking you into thinking that they are well rooted, but this top growth may be just from the sap contained in the cutting, so don't be tempted to shift them until you are sure that the roots are growing strongly.

You will see them growing out of the bottom of the pot sometimes. If you *must* have a look, turn the pot over on to your hand, fingers between the cuttings and see if the roots are formed. If they are, well and good; you can pot them up, but if not, just replace the pot and cuttings and minimal disturbance will have taken place.

When the cuttings are in the rooting medium, it is *most important* that you do not feed them at all. The roots will grow down in their search for food, and that's exactly what you want on the cutting; roots, not top growth. You can feed the potted up cuttings, but it is best to use a little compost scratched into the soil, as inorganic fertilisers can burn the fragile new root systems.

When potting the cuttings up to larger pots, do handle them very carefully, and make the potting mix just a little less rich than usual by the addition of some of the cutting medium. There is plenty of time for a richer mix when you again pot them up to larger containers.

Planting out into garden beds can be done in the following winter, or whenever you decide that your new plants are strong enough. Remember that they must have moist soil to survive. Experience is your best teacher in this process, so take lots of cuttings at different times of the year and experiment with different mixes till you find the way that suits you best.

Layering

Layering is not often used as a method of rose propagation as it requires flexible canes that can be bent to the ground and fixed there, and the canes of many modern roses are too firm and strong to allow this. But layering is a very successful method and suits Climbers and Ramblers and any other cultivars with a lax growth habit.

Find a straight piece of cane that will allow itself to be bent easily to the ground. A steaming bowl of hot water under the cane for a minute or two will help to make the cane more flexible while you complete the operation. With a knife, scrape along the underside of the cane for several centimetres, preferably including the area immediately below some growth eyes. You can dust a hormone powder on to this scraped part if you like. *Do not* cut the cane from the parent plant.

Firm the scraped part of the cane into the soil and cover with 2 or 3 cm of soil. It is a good idea to use pumice here, or whatever medium you use for striking cuttings. It is essential that it drains freely. You may need to peg the cane down with some strong wire from a coat hanger, or you can place some pieces of rock on top to hold it firm in the soil and prevent it springing back up again as soon as you turn your back!

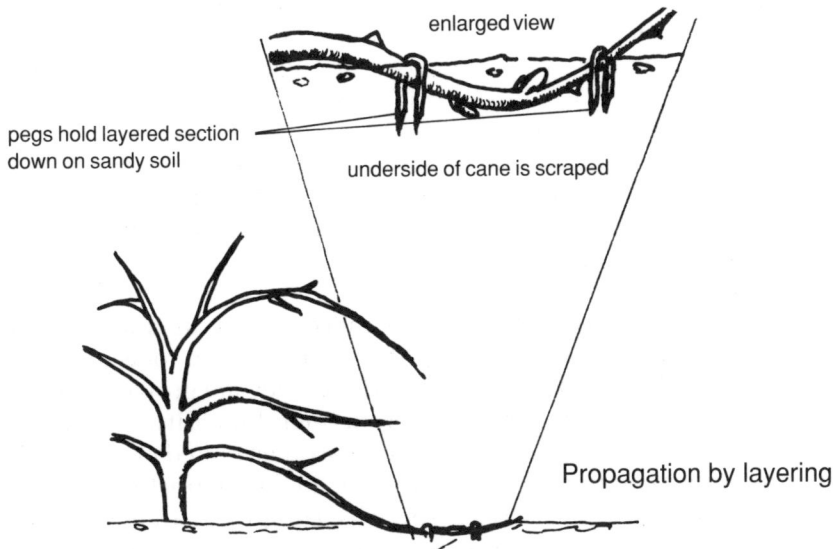

enlarged view

pegs hold layered section down on sandy soil

underside of cane is scraped

Propagation by layering

flexible cane bent down to ground level and held in place with pegs

Trim off all the leaves from the layered part, water in gently and keep the soil moist for a month or two. Then, when some strong new growth is evident from the layered part, scratch gently around to see if roots have formed. If not, just cover the layer again and water in and try in another month or two. If there is a good root system, you can cut the layer away from the parent plant, close to where the root mass has formed. Leave the new plant where it is for a while, a month or so, then if all is well, it can be gently lifted and planted in its own permanent site. When growing plants from cuttings or by layering, do not be in too much of a hurry to move the new plants on.

Tissue culture

Tissue culture is being used increasingly for commercial plant propagation. It is particularly useful when nurserymen have only small numbers of a plant that they wish to increase rapidly, as hundreds of plants can be produced from a very small amount of propagating material. Tissue culture is undertaken in laboratories, under sterile conditions.

The initial propagating material can be taken from various parts of the plant, depending on the species; e.g., from the growing tip, from buds in the leaf axils, from roots, or from dormant buds in bulbs. The 'mother plant' must be grown in controlled conditions to ensure that the material has a very low microbe population. The propagating material, commonly called an explant, is sterilised and placed in an agar gel medium and fed on a complex and precise mixture of nutrients. Light, humidity and temperature are all precisely controlled.

The explant will develop a shoot and it is then fed hormones called cytokinins so that the number of shoots multiplies rapidly. These shoots can be used as new propagating material, or they can be taken on to the next stage.

If processed on, rooting hormones called auxins are added to the nutrient mix in order to encourage the shoots to form roots and they then become tiny plants in their own right. They are grown on in the laboratory, under mist or fog, providing high humidity, and with a gradual increase in light. The small plants are then potted up in a sterile mix and grown on until they are available to the contractor.

Tissue culture is expensive, as specialist equipment, trained technicians, and a large amount of research and development are required, but it is the fastest way of propagating a large number of plants. This technique can also be used to remove viruses from plants, and once the plants are 'cleaned up', the High Health status can then be maintained in the cultures indefinitely. This enables nurserymen to transport plant material internationally with the minimum of quarantine problems.

Tissue culture can be used to change or mutate plants, and so is in the forefront of the genetic engineering technology currently being used to create new varieties of plants. Roses grown by tissue culture do not need to be budded, as they are growing on their own roots, but of course they may be used later for budwood or for cuttings to propagate further plants in more familiar ways.

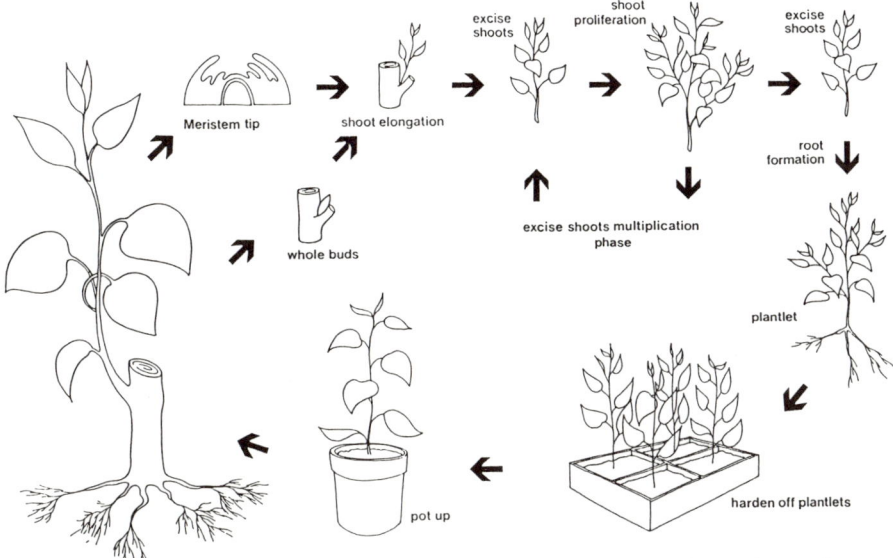

Tissue culture flow chart
Reproduced by kind permission of
Lifetech Laboratories, Auckland, New Zealand

Budding

This is the preferred method of propagation for most commercial nurserymen. In many cases, the plants thus produced will grow larger than cutting grown plants. Some nurseries offer both cutting grown and budded plants. Many Old roses seem to be more readily grown from cutting than from budding. With budding, however, nurseries are able to bud many more plants of a cultivar in short supply than they could grow as cuttings, given the same amount of material with which to propagate. Budding only requires one growth eye per plant, and using budwood for cuttings can 'waste' valuable buds.

Rosa multiflora is the rootstock of choice for most nurseries. It is strong, easily budded and transplants readily, as well as striking well from cuttings, thus ensuring a supply of understocks for future budding. It is possible to obtain plants of *R. multiflora* and try your hand at budding. Watching an experienced budder makes the process look ridiculously easy and theoretically it is a simple process, but it does take some practice! A sharp budding knife and a strong back are needed if you plan on budding more than just a very few plants. There is no reason not to have a try though, and there is tremendous satisfaction when your bud 'takes'.

A single plant of *R. multiflora* will provide you with lots of rootstock cuttings, so plant one somewhere in the garden against the day when you get the urge to bud a few roses. The cuttings for later budding are grown in the way described earlier for cuttings, but all growth eyes below the budded area must be eventually cut out to prevent suckering.

Budding is a summer operation, and it is advisable to have the sap flowing freely in the understock plants, so ample watering in the week or two before budding is recommended. As budding only requires one bud, the bud should be selected carefully. Bud eyes are found in the angle between the leaf and the stem on young wood. The top eyes may not be sufficiently developed, so select one from lower down.

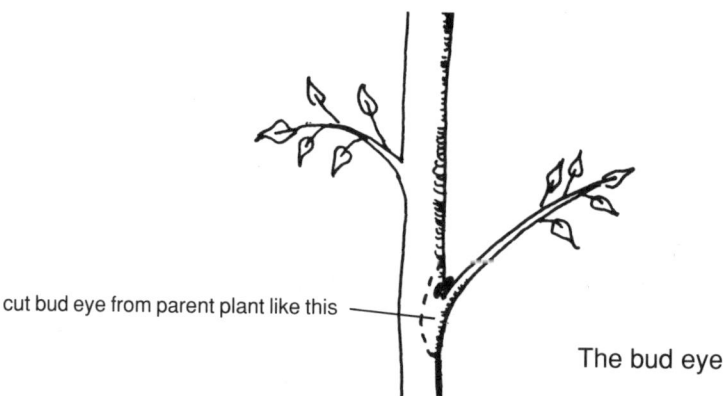

cut bud eye from parent plant like this

The bud eye

Budding can be carried out in some areas as early as November, and performing the operation then will allow for another attempt later in the summer if the first one should prove unsuccessful. A sharp budding knife is essential and you will needs strips of plastic, rubber or raffia for tying in the buds. Budwood is ready for use when the thorns will snap off easily from the stem, and you can usually get three suitable buds from a piece of stem about the same size as is used for cuttings, i.e., 20 cm.

Stems for budwood may be cut and kept in water until you are ready to use them. You will be able to handle the budwood more easily if the thorns are broken off and any leaves cut off.

Cut into the bark of the bud stick about 2 cm above the eye, then cut downwards, just deeply enough to remove the bud with a little of the next layer, the cambium, attached to it. Finish the cut about 2 cm below the eye. The cut-out pieces should be a shield shape with the bud in the centre. This piece is now called the bud shield or plate. A short piece of soft leaf stalk left on the shield will make it easier to handle.

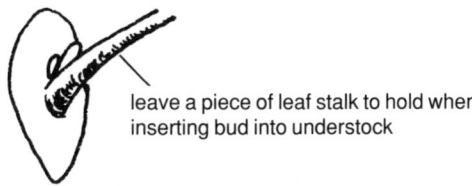

leave a piece of leaf stalk to hold when inserting bud into understock

Bud shield

Next, make a T-shaped incision in the bark of the rootstock at the level you choose, usually about 8 cm above the root mass. Make the horizontal part of the T-cut about 3 cm long and the vertical one about 5 cm. Make these cuts just deep enough to slit the bark without cutting into the cambium layer, which is the shiny layer that you will see under the bark.

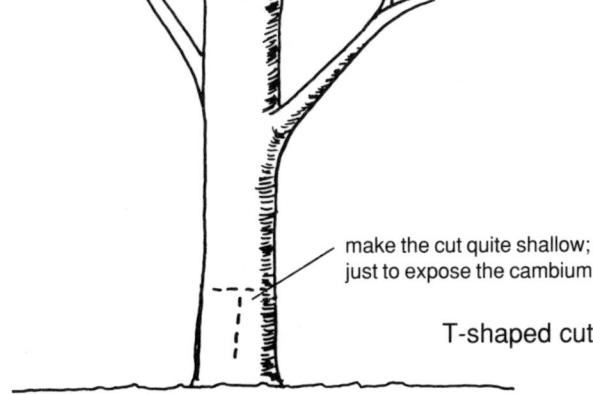

make the cut quite shallow; just to expose the cambium

T-shaped cut

Now gently lift the flaps of the T so that you can slide the bud shield into the incision. Force the shield into the incision gently but firmly, cutting off the top part of the shield to make it level with the horizontal cut. The main part of the shield should now be fitted into the space behind the flaps of bark.

Now tie the shield in place by binding the bark flaps over it with the prepared ties. Do *not* cover the eye itself, but bind firmly above and below it. Tie off firmly, aiming to keep the bud in contact with the cambium layer of the rootstock. Attach a label with the name of the budded cultivar.

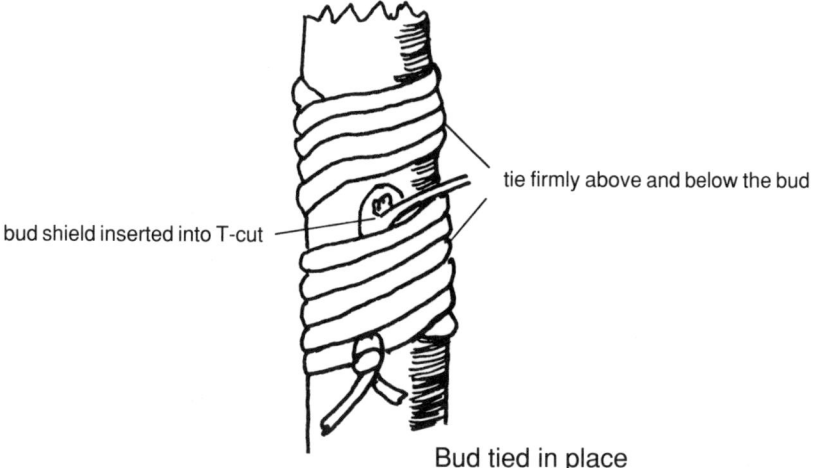

tie firmly above and below the bud

bud shield inserted into T-cut

Bud tied in place

In about three weeks, if the budding has been a success, the bud eye will begin to increase in size, showing that it has 'taken'. A little later, the ties can be cut away and the understock can have its top cut right back, including any eyes that were on it. Keep the budded plant's roots moist and the bud will continue to grow. The new union between rootstock and bud will remain quite frail for some months, so it is advisable to stake the plant carefully to avoid the bud being knocked out or blown out by strong winds.

When the new growth from the bud union is about 10 cm long, it can be lightly trimmed by cutting off the top 2 or 3 cm. The bud union may then throw out some new basal shoots, making a bushier plant and stronger union. It is often advisable to leave the newly budded plant where it is for 12 months to avoid damage to the bud union, but budded plants can be lifted and planted in their selected places the following winter.

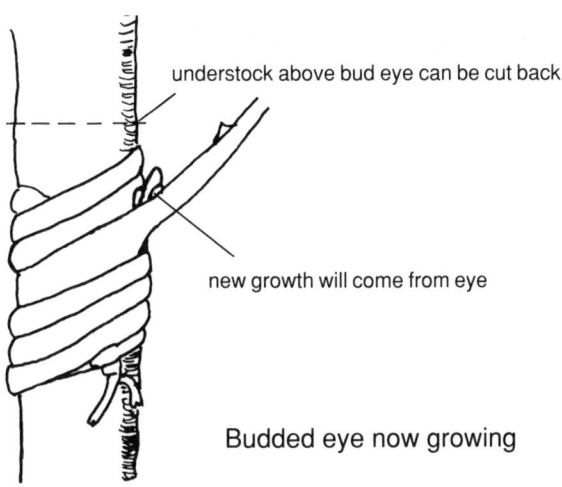

understock above bud eye can be cut back

new growth will come from eye

Budded eye now growing

8 Hybridising

In the search for definite attributes in garden roses,
fortunate chance has to combine with endless care in planning,
recording and much hard labour.

Allen Paterson [5]

It would be impossible to write a chapter on hybridising without
mentioning the work of Sam McGredy. Sam, the fourth generation of
his family to raise roses, migrated to New Zealand from Ireland in 1972.
Since that time, he has introduced no less than 96 new cultivars to the
rose world. He is a most prolific hybridist and most gardeners, whether
they are aware of it or not, have at least some of Sam McGredy's roses
in their gardens.

Sam lives in Auckland, and here in the Southern Hemisphere we are
very fortunate in that we are the first to receive his new releases, and
have them flourishing them in our gardens long before the rest of the
world has them. Sam won't be drawn on his favourite rose, saying that
it hasn't been raised yet, but will admit to some that he wishes he had
raised (see page 88, Chapter 10). The awards that Sam's roses have
received are probably beyond counting, but it would not be too much
to say that he is one of the world's leading hybridists.

Hybridising is the method by which new roses are created, and
hybridizers put enormous amounts of time and effort into researching
the ancestors of their parent plants in order to breed specific characteristics into their new roses. We can see that roses set seeds, by the
appearance of heps on the plants after the flowers have fallen. These
heps that we see are 'open pollinated', meaning that the pollen which
fertilised the ova of the seed parent or 'mother', may or may not have
been from another cultivar. These randomly pollinated heps will
certainly produce viable seeds, but the hybridizer wants to select his or
her own pollen parents for colour, flower shape, resistance to disease,
growth habit, fragrance, or any other desired characteristics, to combine with the characteristics of the seed parent.

English roses (David Austin)
Above: 'Wenlock'
Right: 'Graham Thomas'
Below: 'Ellen'

Floribundas
Left: 'French Lace'
Above: 'Friesia'
Right:
'Hot Chocolate'

Miniatures
Above: 'Rosie'
Left: 'Starglo'
Below: 'Jean Keneally'

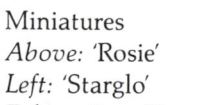

Many fine roses have, however, been grown from randomly pollinated seed, and it is interesting to grow these seeds just to see what comes up. If this aspect of rose growing appeals, you could join your local amateur Rose Breeders Association and you will then be able to benefit from the advice and experience of those who have been hybridising for some time. The roses that you grow from seed may not be of world class, but they will be original, totally your own, and totally unique!

The work of the professional hybridizer is a great deal more serious, and the results can make or break a reputation. Introducing a new rose commercially is a costly business and the professional will not introduce a new rose until completely satisfied with its performance.

Growing roses from seed is a relatively simple process, nature has done it unaided for millions of years, but growing commercially viable cultivars is another matter entirely. Breeders spend many years, sometimes generations, perfecting their craft, as a look at the famous rose breeding families of Meilland, Dot, Harkness and McGredy will show. Breeders raise many thousands of seedlings every year, very few of which will ever make the commercial market; in fact far less than 1% of seedlings raised will have what it takes to be a commercial prospect.

The information that follows is included for its interest to gardeners, as another facet of their rose growing interest. The odds against producing a top rose are very long indeed, but amateurs *do* breed some great roses, and it's very satisfying watching your 'own' roses grow. Waiting for that first flower is an incredible experience!

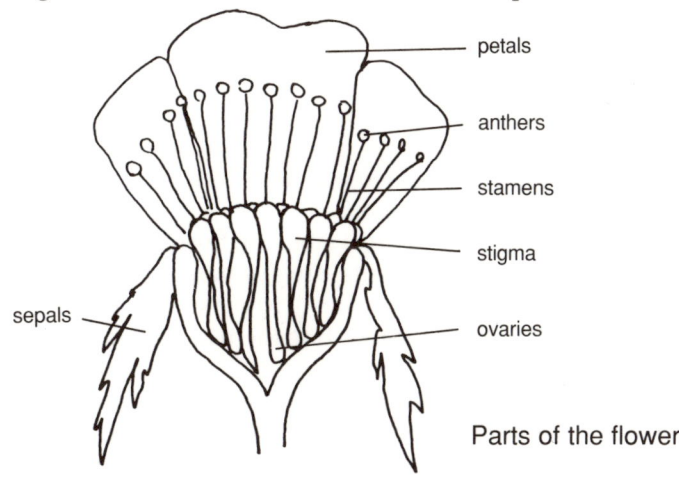

petals

anthers

stamens

stigma

sepals

ovaries

Parts of the flower

You will see from your own roses that some cultivars will set lots of heps and others none at all. Choose then, for the seed parent, one that sets heps readily. Of course, if you carefully dead-head all of the faded flowers there won't be any heps left! So for hybridising, leave the flowers to fade and drop their petals as they do naturally.

Pollinating is best done from spring into early summer to give the heps time to ripen by about May, but local climate variations need to be taken into account, the pollinating season being longer in warm areas. Select a dry, still day for the work if you have to do it outside, and the very early morning is a good time.

Having selected the plant to be the seed parent, you will need to judge when a flower on that plant is ready to be pollinated. When the flower is about two-thirds open, cut off all but the outer circle of petals, and cut off the stamens, being careful not to let pollen from the stamens drop on to the stigma, as this will cause self-pollination.

Stamens from the selected pollen parent can be removed from their flowers in the same way and stored in an open, dry jar or between sheets of white paper. Do label the collected stamens, as the pollen can be used for some weeks or even months. The pollen is ripe when it sheds from the anthers and this may be as soon as a few hours on a warm day.

You can apply the pollen to the stigma of the seed parent with a small paintbrush or a cotton bud or just a moistened fingertip. Whatever 'implement' you use, make sure to clean it when you change to a different pollen. When you can see through a magnifying glass that the stigma is glistening, you will know that it is ripe and ready for pollination. If you are unable to see the stigma glistening, apply the ripe pollen anyway, immediately after removing the petals and stamens from the seed parent. Some people emasculate the seed parent's flowers totally; removing all petals and stamens, then, using a short, thin stake and wire, suspend the pollen parent, with petals also removed, over the stigma of the seed parent. The pollen will then drop as it ripens and will be absorbed when the stigma ripens.

When you have made the cross, do label the flower head of the seed parent with the name of both parents, always naming the seed parent first. This means that you will not need to make a new label when stratifying the seeds later or when planting them in boxes in spring. Use waterproof labels and pens.

If your cross is successful, the hep will start to swell in a couple of weeks and will ripen by the end of the growing season, ready to be harvested around May. Sadly some heps will shrivel and die after swelling promisingly, so it's as well to make plenty of crosses to ensure at least some viable seeds. Do keep up the fungicide spray as the heps are ripening. When the heps have changed to yellow, orange or red, they are ready to be harvested; the stems should still look green and healthy.

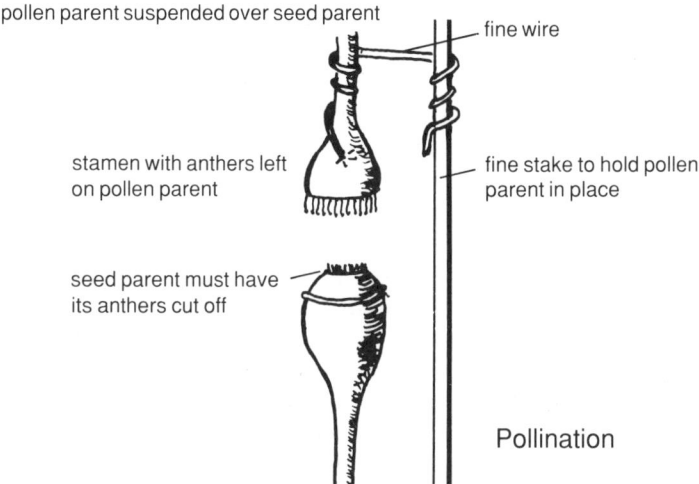

pollen parent suspended over seed parent

fine wire

stamen with anthers left on pollen parent

fine stake to hold pollen parent in place

seed parent must have its anthers cut off

Pollination

After harvesting, the seeds will need to be stratified (kept cold for a period of time). The simplest method is to remove the seeds from the heps with a sharp knife. Some will yield many seeds and some only one or two. Some people 'float test' the seeds, discarding ones that float and keeping the 'sinkers' as they are more likely to germinate, but this method is not really reliable as a certain indicator of viability as seeds that float often *do* germinate.

Place the seeds on damp paper and wrap it around them, then put them in a plastic bag in the refrigerator, *not* the freezer. The period of refrigeration varies, some growers advocating just three or four weeks, but most people leave the seeds there until August when it is time to sow. It is necessary to keep the seeds damp as this helps to soften the testa, or seed coat, making germination easier. Do put the name tags in with the seeds in the bag!

In early spring, the seeds can be sown about 25 mm deep and 25 mm apart in a deep container, or directly into seed beds. A deep container is better than a shallow one (optimally, 15 cm deep, to allow for good root formation), as transplanting seedlings can cause some losses, and the deep container means that you won't need to transplant them quite so early. Make sure the containers have plenty of drain holes, too. Use a seed raising mix, and if not already treated, it should be sprayed with a fungicide to prevent the seedlings 'damping off' (a fungal infection that causes seedling to wither and die).

It can be useful to have your seed containers up off the ground, perhaps at waist height to save lots of bending when you are watching closely for germination. It will also protect the seedlings somewhat better from slugs and snails. If cats or birds are a problem, cover the seed boxes with wire mesh. Keep the mix moist and within a few weeks some of the seeds will germinate. Some will take longer, and others may not emerge until the next year, so don't throw away the ones that don't emerge straight away.

The first pair of leaves to emerge will not look in the least like rose leaves, but the third one and others will have the familiar serrations. When the seedlings have a few 'real' leaves, they can be potted on to individual pots, but it won't hurt to delay this a little till the plants are stronger, as long as the seedlings are not crowding each other. If you get around 40% germination you are doing well.

Watch for signs of damping off. A fungicide will help to prevent this, but so does outside germination with free air circulation. Allow the seedlings more light as they grow, and keep them growing strongly by potting them on to bigger pots and feeding them lightly with a liquid food sprayed on at half the normal strength. Protect them from pests and diseases.

Remember that roses love the sun, but don't overdo it when the little plants are at the tender stage. Get them used to it gradually, especially if they have germinated indoors. As the weather warms up, the plants will keep growing and buds will form. This is the most exciting time; waiting to see what you've created. To have come this far through all of the potential hazards, makes all the fiddly work worthwhile.

The first flowers may not be up to much, and may have very few petals, but wait for the second flowering which often produces much better blooms. If you are strong-minded enough, you will eventually discard any that are obviously weak or have malformed flowers, and this really *is* necessary. With healthy plants, however, grow them on for a season or two and see what happens.

All of this experimenting will fill you with admiration for the professional breeders who go through this process every year in order to raise the wonderful roses that we sometimes take for granted in our own gardens. If by a miracle, you produce what looks to you to be a really good rose, it can be patented and sold commercially. By patenting, new roses are protected by copyright, and the breeder is then assured of continuing royalties on further propagation of roses that he or she has raised. Others who wish to propagate that rose commercially must pay a royalty to the agent appointed by the breeder to collect this fee. Royalties are paid at a set rate for cuttings and buds taken, whether they grow or not.

It is not permitted to propagate roses for sale that are still protected by a patent unless royalties are paid, and most nurseries will give information regarding those cultivars that are still under patent in their catalogues, usually by the letter P or PP somewhere in the cultivar lists.

Amateur rose growers who have raised some of their own roses via hybridization could try budding some of them on to understock to see how they fare. Many will produce better blooms and be of stronger growth habit when grown in this way.

Keep experimenting with all of the aspects of rose culture. The more you discover through your own experience, the better. Many fine roses have been raised by amateurs and there is no reason at all why more gardeners cannot experience the fascination of hybridising.

Sports

A sport is a mutation or change in an existing cultivar. For reasons not yet fully understood, one branch of a plant may be different in some way from the rest of the plant. It may suddenly become a climber, or the flowers can be of a different colour or shape from the others on the rest of the parent plant. Because of the tendency of some cultivars to sport a climbing cane, growers are able to propagate from that cane and so enable many cultivars to be purchased in either Bush or Climbing form.

If cuttings or buds are taken from the sport, then an entirely new rose can be patented in the way described above. Some cultivars, for example the Miniature 'Pink Petticoat', are noted for their ability to keep producing sports, and sporting can happen in any garden with any rose. While the fortunate discoverer and patenter of a sport cannot truly be said to have created that rose, sports are recognised as new roses and patented as such.

Roses from overseas sources

New cultivars from overseas are being introduced to the local market every year. The introduction of new cultivars is not a simple procedure and can only be undertaken under the rules that are laid out for plant material in general, and roses specifically as a genus. The process is strictly controlled.

Firstly, a Permit to Import is required and accompanying the propagating material must be an International Health Certificate from the country of export. On arrival, the plant material is examined for pests and diseases. It must arrive packed in an approved sterile medium, e.g., sphagnum moss or damp newspaper, so that no undesirable bacterial matter is present.

If given a health clearance, the plant material is then released to the premises of the importer to be held under strict quarantine control. The propagating material, usually bud eyes, sometimes cuttings, is then inspected two or three times in each growing season for the next two years, after which, if cleared, it can be released for sale.

9 Monthly maintenance

*A gardener's life
Is full of sweets and sours;
He gets the sunshine
When he needs the showers.
But don't forget
He's always growing flowers.*
Reginald Arkell

The following is a guide to maintenance for central districts. Allowances must be made for the far north or the far south, work generally being carried out earlier in the north and later in the south. In general, the timing of maintenance tasks is not crucial, so there is plenty of room for leeway either side of the suggested times. If in doubt, consult a local rose society. This routine maintenance applies to all types of roses.

April

It is difficult to decide just when to start the rose year, but April is the time for deciding on and preparing new beds, enriching the soil, deciding on placement of new roses and removing plants that are to be replaced.

If not already done, roses should be ordered from nurseries by now and it is a good time to plant out well-rooted cuttings taken late in summer or to pot them up in good soil.

For new beds, break the soil up thoroughly and incorporate lots of humus and matured compost. If compost is not available, use plenty of blood and bone instead. Allowing the beds to lie fallow for a time will help the composition of the soil and allow earthworms to do their valuable work. If you are short of earthworms, as can be the case in a new garden or in previously unworked heavy soils, check under pots outside, in piles of vegetation in gutters and under trees. Your compost heap should prove a good source of earthworms too, as they will come up into it from deep in the soil. You can also buy earthworms and have them sent to you by mail.

In established gardens, if you have given your roses a summer trim, you will be rewarded now by some of the best roses of the year. They will last longer than spring blooms and there will be more of them because the plants are so much bigger.

Spraying is needed to prevent black spot and mildew. There may still be aphids about and these need to be kept under control. You will need a suitable sprayer. There are many types available and size will depend on how many roses you have. It is best to purchase a sprayer larger than you need initially as rose gardens have a tendency to expand dramatically as the gardener gets well and truly 'hooked'!

May

Check the beds newly turned last month and remove any weeds that have germinated. Re-work the soil to make it more friable. Spray roses again if diseases are a problem, but in the south, cooler weather will put an end to most pests and diseases.

This is the time to practise good hygiene in the rose beds. Gather up and burn all fallen leaves as a protection against the carry over of disease on to the next season's growth. Many disease fungi will winter over on fallen leaves, so it is really important that this material is burned and not *ever* incorporated into the compost heap.

The plants will be approaching dormancy now, so there will be no need to water or feed unless conditions are extremely dry. You should still be able to pick lots of roses from repeat flowering cultivars.

It is too early to prune, but a good time to spread a thick mulch over both new and existing beds to further improve the condition and content of the soil. Just allow the mulch to lie on top of the beds; there is no need to dig it in.

Start to collect ripened heps if you want to try growing roses from seed. Cuttings of roses may still be taken.

June

This is a good time to begin planting new roses as they become available as bare root bushes, but many nurseries do not lift their plants until late in June or into July. Make sure that all plants to be discarded have been removed and that you have burned any that were badly affected by disease. Good plants that are just not to your liking can be swapped with friends in the same predicament. Most people want to try a new cultivar from time to time and consigning a perfectly good plant to the incinerator seems a waste when you could find it a good home.

Plants that you want to move can be shifted this month. But, be sure to plant them in new soil (see page 37). Cut back plants that you are shifting in order to facilitate handling, but leave 'proper' pruning until July.

Spray to kill any aphids or mites that are still lurking about. This spray should also cause the plants to drop their remaining leaves and go into a dormant state. Lime sulphur or a copper and oil spray should be used at this time of the year. You can delay this application if the roses are still blooming.

July

Keep planting new roses as they arrive or as you 'fall' for the picture of yet another cultivar in the garden centre. If you are unable to plant at once, 'heel in' the plants (see page 36).

July is pruning time for most rose growers, but the exact time will depend on the area in which you live. Prune early in the month in warm areas and later, even into August, in areas that experience heavy frosts. In these frost-prone areas, pruning too early can mean that new growth is killed by a late, heavy frost. Do your own pruning ... no-one else can do it better. Whatever your pruning experience or style, the result will still be more roses from spring to autumn, so there is no need to panic if you feel that you don't know enough about it yet.

Cuttings may be still be taken in July, and since you are pruning anyway, there's nothing to lose by trying a few.

Another dormant spray, lime sulphur if you used copper and oil last time and vice versa, can be applied this month to eliminate spores of black spot, mildew and rust.

There's no point in watering this month, except to thoroughly soak newly planted roses. Feeding is not recommended at this time. Many plants will be showing new growth in warmer areas.

Check established Climbers and Standards to see that all ties are firm, and replace any that have rotted or are too tight.

August

If you budded any cultivars on to rootstock in the summer, now is a good time to cut back the understock. Finish your planting and pruning this month if you didn't quite make it in July.

By now everything should be planted, pruned, sprayed and tidied up ready for the new season's growth. You can feed your roses later in the month with a complete rose food, superphosphate or blood and bone if the new shoots are coming away well, but leave the feeding until September in colder areas. Do not feed newly planted roses at all.

Late in August, check the plants you have pruned to see that you have cut to an eye that is actually developing, (see page 48). If the top eye has failed to develop, cut to a lower one. If you want to keep the centre of the plant open, you can rub out with your finger any eyes that are facing in that way.

This is the month to remove your rose seeds from the refrigerator and sow them, dreaming of the wonderful new roses you have created from hybridizing. August is definitely a month for dreaming, especially if leaden skies and continual rain keep you indoors.

Re-tie Climbers and Ramblers if you pruned them back hard in July. Draw the lower canes down close to the horizontal and tie them in firmly (see page 50).

September

If you did not feed your roses in August, do so this month, but not the ones newly planted in winter. According to the area in which you live, there will be great variation in the amount of growth on the plants now. In the warmest areas, there may be some early blooms, while central areas will have well developed foliage and buds, and in the south new growth will be appearing.

It is at this time that early pests and diseases can make an appearance, so do spray with a fungicide as a protection against fungus diseases like black spot, especially if the weather is becoming more humid. Aphids will be seen on the new growth, so dispose of them at once, and watch for caterpillars, too, as they can cause damage to soft, young foliage.

You may need to water this month, especially for the new plants, and the soil will be starting to warm up. If you did not mulch your beds in May, do so now after feeding. A 7-cm layer of mulch is ideal; preferably an organic mulch such as compost, grass clippings, or shredded newspaper (as these will decompose slowly, forming part of the soil).

Where you have your rose seeds in pots, you can expect erratic germination now, so keep the mix moist. It may be necessary to spray the emerging seedlings with a fungicide to prevent diseases which will quickly kill the tiny plants, and, yes, the aphids will attack these little ones too, so be on guard.

Remember to keep your cuttings moist and deal with any weeds that appear with the warming of the soil. Roses growing in containers will need a top up or replacement of some of the soil in the containers, as the plants' need for nutrients increases at this time of the year. A layer of mulch is, of course, beneficial for container grown plants, too.

October

By now plants will be really growing fast, and some areas will be experiencing strong winds. If this is so in your garden, you may need to stake and tie in new sappy growths from the bud union (basal shoots) to prevent them being torn off at the base by the wind.

If rainfall is insufficient, plants may need some long, deep waterings. New plants will benefit from some feeding now, but make it a light one, and preferably of organic material, blood and bone or compost.

In warm areas, there will be blooms now in increasing numbers. Blooms may be picked as you like. In the case of roses planted only last winter, cut the blooms with just short stems, and as individual flowers fade dead-head them at once. If, as you cut each flower, you cut the stem just above a leaf with five leaflets, a new flower will grow from the bud eye in about six weeks. This, of course, only applies to repeat flowering cultivars, but is worth remembering every time you want to cut blooms; a sort of 'mini pruning' which can be carried on throughout the flowering season.

October and November are ideal times to start visiting rose nurseries and rose gardens as there will be lots of blooms and you will be inspired to make your selections for next year's beds or for replacement bushes in existing beds.

Continue spraying fungicide as new growth develops. When you are spraying, take care not to spray in windy weather. All spraying should be done on calm, still days to avoid spray drift, and avoid the hottest part of the day. It is advisable to wear protective clothing, too. Seedlings will benefit from weak applications of fungicide and systemic pesticide, as they are not yet strong plants.

Keep your mulch loose with a hoe and do not allow the mulch to compact down as it may then prove an impenetrable barrier to water.

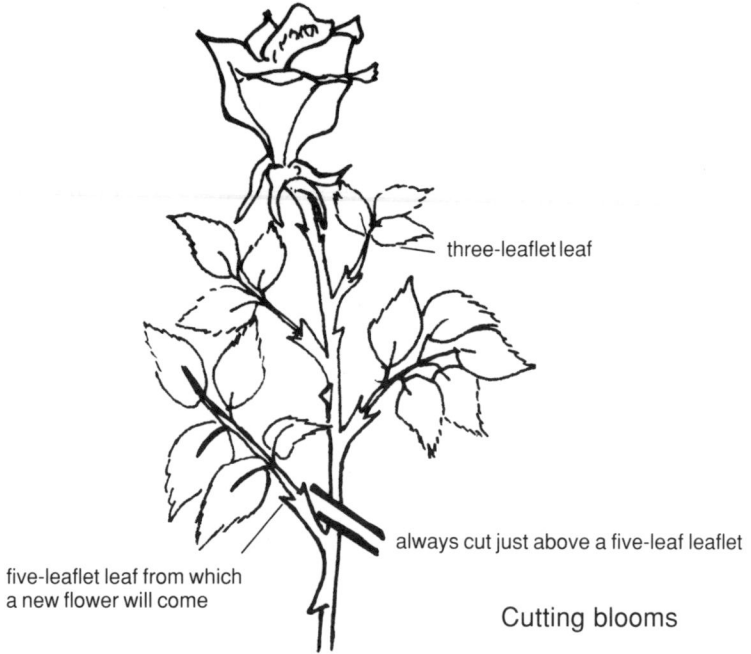

three-leaflet leaf

always cut just above a five-leaf leaflet

five-leaflet leaf from which
a new flower will come

Cutting blooms

November

Most areas will now be in the big spring flush of bloom, repaying the care that has been given to the plants. Foliage will be lush and hopefully you will be encouraged by the appearance of 'watershoots' or basal shoots (new growths from the bud union) which will provide the framework for the subsequent year's growth. Stake and tie these if wind is a factor.

Continue to cut off faded flower heads, and trim off any twiggy growth that appears from the bud union to encourage the plant to use its resources on good basal shoots, rather than expending it on weak growth that will not come to much.

If you want to try growing roses from seed, allow some heps to ripen, but otherwise keep removing them, as ripening heps will hinder further flower production. Try some hybridizing now.

A very light feeding after the first flush of bloom will be beneficial, and if the soil is kept moist, another flush of blooms will come in December.

Keep up the fungicide spraying to prevent black spot, which can get a really good hold now, especially in humid weather. As black spot cannot be cured, it must be prevented. It can quickly defoliate a plant and spread to others via wind blown spores or contact. Spray your little seedlings, too, and protect them from the ravages of disease and of aphids, snails and slugs.

If you plan to enter some of your roses in a show, you may decide to 'disbud' some cultivars. This involves removing all but the terminal flower bud, so that the remaining flower's size and quality will be improved. Do visit the shows if you can; they are a reliable source of information about which roses do well in your area. The local rose society will have the details of dates and venues and be able to supply you with a show schedule which tells you the classes you may enter.

Your cuttings will be shooting well and must still be kept moist. Some may be ready to pot up to grow on. Check for roots growing out the bottom of the pot before you up-end them. Pot each one up individually in small, deep pots and give them a bit more sun, but do it gradually.

December

Continue to water if needed. A really good soak once a week is much better than light sprinklings, and will keep the plants growing strongly and flowering well. Keep dead-heading faded flowers. Renew mulch if needed to prevent moisture from evaporating.

Keep the fungicide and insecticide spray going, possibly every ten days or so in warmer, humid areas. Rust may appear on the undersides of leaves, and if rust or black spot attacks a plant badly, pick off and burn all the affected foliage and spray the plant again to prevent a recurrence. A really bad infection may require surgery. Cut off entire canes if necessary to halt the spread of the disease. The plant will suffer less from radical surgery than if it is left with diseased canes. Some plants, if they continue to be affected should be dug out and abandoned, as there are certainly some cultivars that do not resist disease as well as others.

Continue to hybridize throughout December and well into January. If the crosses are successful, the heps will swell in a few weeks. Leave them on the plants, affixing the name of both parents.

When cutting roses in summer, cut them very early in the morning, and steep them in tepid water in a cool place for a few hours before arranging. Otherwise, cut in late afternoon or evening when it is cooler.

Save the rose petals and dry them for pot pourri, etc.; you can do this all the flowering season (see Using your roses, Chapter 12).

January

It's time to make a choice: do you allow your roses to keep blooming, or do you sacrifice some blooms now for the sake of a really good autumn flush?

If the former is your choice, keep dead-heading, give the plants plenty of water and a somewhat heavier feeding in late January. Blood and bone with the addition of some potassium sulphate is advised (be sure to read the manufacturers' instructions on all products).

Spray again for black spot and insect pests and watch for the unwelcome appearance of mildew, a whitish powdery coating on the foliage of plants, especially where they grow in the protection of house eaves or anywhere that free circulation of air is impeded.

If you decide to trim the plants for an autumn blooming, you can withhold water from the plants after Christmas. Cut blooms you want for the house with only short stems, but always still to a strong growth eye. Do keep the spray programme going and when cutting spent flowers, just cut off the heads, leaving the stems, as they will be trimmed next month.

Remember to keep potted roses moist; this is one case where daily watering may be essential if the plants are on sunny decks and patios, but do water deeply each time.

January and February are the months when roses are budded on to rootstock, and you could try doing this (see Chapter 7). Keep hybridizing and keep an eye out for spider mites. They will hide under the leaves and can be disposed of by a good, strong hosing, but be sure to hose under the leaves.

February

Keep staking and tying in basal shoots and keep up the spray programme this month. If you are not trimming for an autumn display, keep watering your plants. If you *have* decided to trim for autumn blooming, now is the time for the trim (see page 52).

Having trimmed, water the beds generously and follow with another feeding; this time with extra potash. Top up the mulch layer and water heavily again. The plants need lots of food now if they are to give good autumn blooms. Any added compost that you incorporate into the mulch will be part of the soil before winter comes. Keep the beds moist until the blooms start to appear; this is very important. Nature will supply the warmth that the plants need to bloom in autumn, but you must supply the water.

Keep the surface of the beds loose and keep at the weeds that will have been pleased to receive all that extra food and water, too.

Trim any large, weeping Standard roses and feed them to get new long canes for next year's blooms. For summer trimming, times are vary according to area, but it is worth experimenting to get the timing right. Generally, in central areas, the roses will bloom again 55 to 60 days after the summer trim, so if you have a special date in mind for blooms this gives you a rough guide as to what to expect. In later years, you can adjust the date of the trim according to last year's performance, but practising summer trimming for autumn blooms is always worthwhile.

March

Watch for mildew this month as cooler nights will encourage its growth. Summer trimmed plants will be growing well with help from all the extra food and water. Roses not trimmed will still be blooming this month, but the blooms may be smaller than those in spring. In very warm areas, summer trimming may be done in March. Aphids may again be troublesome and caterpillars sometimes appear, so keep the sprayer going.

Keep watering and staking basal shoots which will grow and have time to mature before you prune in July.

A light feeding now will help the autumn blooms. Perhaps you would prefer to use a foliar feed, applied with your sprayer to the foliage. You can often mix the foliar feed with the fungicide and insecticide you are using, but do be guided by the manufacturer's instructions. Don't overdo the foliar feeding though, as most foliar feeds are high in nitrogen and can cause the foliage to become lush at the expense of flower quality.

Time your watering to coincide with showery weather if possible, and avoid overhead watering in the heat of the day.

Start thinking about next year's beds and dig them over roughly if time and your inclination permit.

April

In established gardens, there will be a glorious flush of blooms from summer trimmed roses. The blooms are of better colour and will last much longer than the spring flowers and there are more of them too, as the plants are bigger.

Keep spraying to catch any late aphids as they can cause sooty mould, a black fungus which grows on the exuded honeydew.

Cutting grown plants can be planted out now if their size permits, otherwise pot them up into larger pots and leave till winter.

For new beds, add lime to acid soil and gypsum to alkaline soil and add compost to improve the content. Dig over if you like, but you can just spread these additives onto the surface and let the rain and worms do the rest.

Heps on fertilised flowers will be swelling now and will be ripening to yellow, orange and red, ready to be harvested in May.

Decide on any plants to be replaced and remove them as soon as possible.

Cuttings can be taken now with a good chance of success. To be certain of getting some to strike, take a few regularly from now till July pruning time.

Having said all of this, it is a pity to see gardeners who are so obsessed by what they feel they *must* do to their plants that they forget why they are growing them in the first place. If you miss a feeding or get some aphids or black spot, it really isn't earth shattering. Remember that you grow roses for *their* beauty and *your* pleasure, so take the time to relax and enjoy them. If you grow your roses in the sun and in good garden soil, they will reward you with blooms. All of the feeding and trimming and spraying are things that you can do to improve your roses, not things that you *must* do to grow roses!

'Handel' (Climbing rose)

Old-fashioned roses
Left: 'Wedding Day'
Above left: 'Cecile Brunner'
Above right:
Rosa rugosa alba

Above left:
'La Reine Victoria'
Above right:
'Chapeau de Napoleon'
Right: 'Pink Sparrieshoop'

Hybrid tea roses
Above left: 'Grandpa Dickson'
Above top: 'Solitaire'
Above: 'Catherine Deneuve'
Below: 'Sylvia'
Left: 'Kronenbourg'

10 Choosing cultivars

Beauty is in the eye of the beholder.
Margaret Wolfe Hungerford

In rose trial grounds all over the world, roses are grown and judged under strict conditions and rules to see how they perform. Each cultivar is usually trialled for two years, and panels of judges visit the grounds every week to report on each plant's progress. Awards are made by the trial grounds each year and the winning breeders can look forward to commercial success and recognition for the winning cultivars.

Breeders from all countries may enter their roses in the trials of other countries and awards from international trial grounds are highly prized. If you are able, visit the trial grounds in the flowering season to see all of the latest roses from around the world. You will be bound to see some cultivars that you 'need' for your own garden, and it is from here that the favourite roses will emerge in years to come.

Reviewing roses

Each year, national and state rose societies review the newer roses on the market. This is usually done by a panel of reporters, mostly ordinary gardeners, each of whom reports on the particular cultivar as it grows in average garden conditions. In this way, a broad picture of the rose's performance in varied growing conditions can be compiled. The reported material is then collated and the results are published in the *Rose Annual*.

The annuals may also list the top roses in each of the categories of Hybrid tea, Floribunda, Climber and Miniature. These reports show each cultivar's popularity in the current season, with reporters sometimes listing good garden roses as well as cultivars with show potential. Every possible aspect of the rose's growth habit is taken into account in the compilation of these lists. Newer cultivars make their way onto the lists as more people grow them, but old favourites are still to be found.

Top cultivars

In the following lists of roses, each cultivar is described only the *first* time it is mentioned, although each may be mentioned several times.

Roses recommended for their disease resistance are indicated by a 'D' and those recommended for their fragrance are denoted by the letter 'F'. Note that disease resistance and to a lesser extent fragrance are affected by growing conditions. Roses that are well fed and watered are less likely to suffer from disease, and roses growing strongly will, if they are fragrant cultivars, give more of their fragrance. Most of the Old-fashioned types listed are, to a greater or lesser extent, fragrant. For more detailed information consult the catalogues issued by the rose nurseries. These details will include size and growth habit.

New Zealand Rose Society top cultivars*

Hybrid teas

1. **'Loving Memory'** Large crimson blooms with lovely shape. **F**
2. **'Sylvia'** Clear rose-pink blooms with long, pointed buds. **F**
3. **'Gold Medal'** Deep gold with tints of orange; good repeat.
4. **'Pascali'** Pure white blooms great for cutting.
5. **'Alexander'** Vermillion blooms, good for picking. **D**
6. **'Precious Platinum'** Deep crimson blooms with reflexing petals. **D**
7. **'Double Delight'** Creamy blooms edged with crimson. **F**
8. **'Velvet Lustre'** Magenta with lighter tonings; glows with colour.
9. **'First Love'** Mauve/pink blooms of decorative shape.
10. **'Grandpa Dickson'** Large blooms of deep yellow with a faint pink edge.

Floribundas

1. **'Raspberry Ice'** Silvery white blooms edged with red.
2. **'Margaret Merrill'** Pearly white with blush centre. **FD**
3. **'Sexy Rexy'** Soft pink blooms in large trusses. **D**
4. **'Iceberg'** Bush smothers itself in white flowers sometimes tinged pink. **D**
5. **'Julischka'** Large trusses of clear red cover the bush.

* 1990-1991

6. **'Friesia'** Brilliant yellow, large blooms that hold colour well. **FD**
7. **'Playboy'** Brilliant orange with scarlet and gold tones.
8. **'Satchmo'** Scarlet blooms deeper red at the edges.
9. **'Strawberry Ice'** Icy white with cerise margins.
10. **'Priscilla Burton'** Light pink to cerise with splashes of colour.

Miniatures

1. **'Cupcake'** Candy pink flowers great for cutting.
2. **'Minnie Pearl'** Light pink with some creamy yellow tones. Well pointed buds. **F**
3. **'Rise 'n' Shine'** Deep gold blooms good for cutting. **F**
4. **'Black Jade'** Deepest red buds with high pointed centres.
5. **'Pink Petticoat'** Large coral pink blooms, creamy white in the centre.
6. **'Cecile Lens'** Beautifully formed buds open to a soft pink bloom.
7. **'Starglo'** White blooms with creamy tones.
8. **'Little Jackie'** A blend of salmon, cream and orange blooms.
9. **'Magic Carrousel'** White blooms with red edges.
10. **'Moonlight Lady'** Creamy white with pink/buff centres. **D**

Climbers

1. **'Dublin Bay'** Large, deep red blooms, repeats well. **F**
2. **'Handel'** Smaller blooms of cream with rosy pink edges.
3. **'Westerland'** Apricot/bronze blooms with salmon tones. **F**
4. **'Breath of Life'** Soft apricot blooms of good shape. **F**
5. **'Compassion'** Salmon pink/apricot blooms good for cutting. **F**
6. **'Swan Lake'** Blooms near white, tinged pink in the centre.

Australian rose societies top cultivars

Australian state rose societies each publish separate lists of favourite cultivars, but the following Australian favourites appear on most state lists.

Hybrid teas

'April Hamer' Creamy-white, tinged pink at edges. **F**
'Chicago Peace' Petals are pinky-yellow with copper tones. **F**
'Diamond Jubilee' Buff corn shade and shapely flower. **F**

'Double Delight'
'Just Joey' Coppery orange with frilled edges. **F**
'Madame A. Meilland/Peace' Big pale yellow blooms with cerise pink
   edges. One of the world's favourite roses. **FD**
'Paradise' Lilac rose bordered ruby red. **FD**
'Pascali'
'Pink Silk' Deepest rose pink. **F**
'Silver Lining' Mid pink shapely blooms. **F**

Floribundas

'Bridal Pink' Soft organdie pink blooms, well formed. **F**
'Elizabeth of Glamis' Shapely salmon pink blooms. **FD**
'Europeana' Dark crimson flowers in trusses. **FD**
'French Lace' Graceful ivary-white shapely blooms, cuts well. **FD**
'Friesia'
'Gold Bunny' Blloms of deepest gold are unfading.
'Iceberg'
'Margaret Merrill'
'Picasso' Trusses of carmine blooms edged white.

Climbers

'Altissimo' Large blood-red single flowers
'Golden Showers' Free blooming with bright yellow flowers.
'Handel'
'Iceberg'
'Nancy Hayward' Deep pink single flowers. Vigorous. **F**

Miniatures

'Beauty Secret' Deepest red, well formed blooms. **F**
'Jean Keneally' Apricot flowers, well formed. **FD**
'Mary Marshall' Peachy apricot blooms. Profuse. **FD**
'Minnie Pearl'
'Pacesetter' Pure white glorious buds.
'Rise 'n' Shine'
'Starina' Vermillion blooms of good shape.
'Tracey Wickham' Bright yellow flowers, edged red.

Some popular Old-fashioned roses

'**Albertine**' Rambler. Free flowering with light pink double blooms.
'**Ballerina**' Hybrid musk. Huge heads of single pink flowers.
'**Blanc Double De Coubert**' Rugosa. Pure white, semi double flowers.
'**Buff Beauty**' Hybrid musk. Rich, apricot yellow blooms in clusters.
'**Cecile Brunner**' Bush or Climber. Chinensis type. Tiny pale pink
flowers of perfect shape. 'The Sweetheart Rose'
'**Celestial**' Alba. Delicate buds and semi double soft pink flowers.
'**Cornelia**' Hybrid musk. Apricot pink flowers with creamy tones.
'**Duchesse De Brabant**' Tea. Double-cupped flowers, clear salmon pink.
'**Frau Dagmar Hastrupp**' Rugosa. Light pink single flowers.
'**Fruhlingsmorgen**' Spinosissima hybrid. Cherry pink single flowers
with long maroon stamens.
'**General Gallienni**' Tea. Flowers change from deep rose red and buff
to lighter red as they open.
'**Gloire De Dijon**' Tea (Climber). Double, quartered flowers of light
salmon/buff.
'**Jean Ducher**' Tea. Cupped flowers of salmon pink shaded yellow.
'**Madame Legras De St. Germain**' Alba. Snowy white flowers flushed
yellow in the centre.
'**Mme Alfred Carriere**' Noisette (Climber). Globular pinkish to white
flowers in clusters.
'**Mme Isaac Pereire**' Bourbon. Large, double flowers of crimson/
purple.
'**Mme Pierre Ogier**' Bourbon. Palest blush pink cupped blooms.
'**Mermaid**' Bracteata Climber. Large, single flowers of clear yellow.
'**Nancy Steen**' Shrub. Flowers are full and soft blush pink with creamy
centres.
'**Penelope**' Hybrid musk. Creamy pink flowers in large clusters.
'**Raubritter**' Macrantha hybrid. Clusters of silvery pink cupped
flowers.
'**Souvenir De La Malmaison**' Bourbon (Climber or Bush). Blush white,
opening flat and quartered.
'**Stanwell Perpetual**' Species hybrid. Cupped buds open to blush pink
flat flowers.
'**Wedding Day**' Rambler. Profuse clusters of single white flowers.

Favourite English roses

'Graham Thomas' Clear yellow double blooms on a lax bush. **F**
'Mary Rose' Clear pink double flowers.
'Wenlock' Deep red blooms, very double. **F**

Popular Hybrid teas

'Aotearoa/New Zealand' Large, creamy pink blooms on long stems. **FD**
'Auckland Metro' Huge creamy white blooms opening to a camellia shape. **FD**
'Berolina' Large, mid-yellow blooms with amber tones. **F**
'Brandy' Long, elegant buds open to golden apricot flowers.
'Catherine Deneuve' Deep salmon blooms that last well on the bush and when picked. **F**
'City of Auckland' Shapely blooms of deep gold and tangerine. **FD**
'Deep Secret' Deep, blackish red, velvety flowers. **F**
'Elina' Lovely flowers of pale, creamy yellow and perfect shape. **D**
'Esmeralda' Glowing rose pink blooms with high centres. **FD**
'First Love' Shapely blooms opening to wide flowers of pale pink with apricot tones.
'Flamingo' Rose pink blooms on strong stems great for cutting.
'Fragrant Cloud' Free flowering dusky geranium blooms. **F**
'Heart Throb' Elegant blooms, peachy-pink tones. Good for cutting. **F**
'Ingrid Bergman' Deep velvety red blooms which last well. **FD**
'Julia's Rose' Incredible parchment coloured flowers with coppery tones. **F**
'Kronenbourg' Large flowers cerise with gold reverse to the petals. **F**
'Lady Rose' Vermillion/clear pink flowers and beautiful buds. **FD**
'Loving Memory' Large, crimson scarlet flowers. **FD**
'Marijke Koopman' Bright satin pink flowers open from long, elegant buds. **F**
'Papa Meilland' Large flowers of deep crimson. **F**
'Remember Me' Coppery Orange flowers with red/yellow tones. **FD**
'Sheer Bliss' Large creamy blooms blushed pink. **F**
'Silver Jubilee' Salmon pink with peach/coppery tones. **D**
'Solitaire' yellow flushed pink with masses of blooms. **FD**
'Sonia Meilland' Unique porcelain rose blooms, great for cutting. **F**
'The World' Huge flowers of cream/apricot with cerise margins. **D**

'Touch of Class' Shapely, pointed buds open to coral blooms shaded salmon. **D**
'West Coast' Large flowers of clear pink on a large bush. **D**
'Whisky' Shapely blooms of deep gold.

Favourite Climbing roses

'Bantry Bay' Clear rose pink blooms of floribunda type.
'City of London' Palest pink with reflexing outer petals. **F**
'Climbing Iceberg' Climbing sport of Floribunda (above).
'Golden Showers'
'Lady Barbara' Tangerine orange with yellow reverse. **F**
'Uetersen' Frilly, deep pink blooms in clusters. **F**
'White Cockade' Double white blooms in profusion.
'Zephirine Drouhin' Semi double bright cerise blooms. Thornless. **F**

Popular Floribundas

'Avalanche' Free flowering bush with creamy white blooms.
'Doris Tysterman' Bright tangerine orange with deeper edges. **FD**
'English Miss' Sprays of soft pink flowers that open flat. **F**
'Hot Chocolate' Unusual russet brown flowers in clusters. **F**
'Madame President' Camellia-shaped blooms of softest rose pink. **D**
'Matangi' Orange toned flowers with silvery white reverse and petal edges.
'Old Port' Full flowers of deep, burgundy purple. **F**
'Regensberg' Abundant pink and white bicoloured flowers with a 'hand-painted' look.
'Ripples' Silvery lilac blooms with frilly petals.
'Softly Softly' Warm rose pink with peach tones. **FD**
'Trumpeter' Brilliantly coloured orange scarlet blooms. **D**
'Vesper' Well shaped blooms in tones of soft orange/brown.

Popular Miniature/Patio roses

'Andrea' (Semi Climber) Deep pink flowers edged silver. **D**
'Cheers' Burnt orange flowers with paler reverse.
'Cinderella' Tiny, soft pink flowers on a small bush. **F**
'Clarissa' Small apricot flowers in clusters.
'Dorola' Clear gold shapely blooms. **D**
'High Stepper' (Climber) Red with yellow reverse.
'Holy Toledo' Unusual apricot/orange.

'Jeanne Lajoie' (Climber) Mid pink flowers with deeper reverse.
'Kaikoura' Orange red and free flowering. **D**
'Kathy Robinson' Deep cerise pink flowers with creamy buff reverse.
'Ko's Yellow' Large yellow blooms tinged with pink. **FD**
'Little Scotch' Creamy buff blooms that are incredibly fragrant. **F**
'Nozomi' Pearl pink single blooms on spreading canes.
'Orange Honey' Orange/yellow blend.
'Over the Rainbow' Golden yellow blooms tinged bright red.
'Patio Jewel' Large crimson/scarlet blooms.
'Patio Pearl' Semi double blooms of creamy pink.
'Peek a Boo' Masses of charming, apricot and peach blooms.
'Perla de Montserrat' Tiny pink buds open to shell pink flowers. **D**
'Pink Delight' Soft shell-pink.
'Popcorn' Small grower with many white flowers in clusters that look
    and smell just like sugared popcorn. **F**
'Rainbow's End' Yellow and scarlet flowers on a vigorous bush. **D**
'Ring of Fire' Yellow flowers, edged orange.
'Sierra Sunrise' Soft yellow and pink.
'Snow Carpet' Ground cover rose with tiny creamy white flowers.
'Starglo' Perfectly formed creamy white flowers.
'Sugar Elf' (Climber) Small pink/gold blend flowers.
'Sunblaze' Bright orange vermillion. **D**
'Sweet Raspberry' Lots of small raspberry red flowers in clusters. **F**
'The Fairy' (Polythana type) Masses of small, double pink flowers. **D**
'Wanaka' Bright orange blooms in clusters. **D**
'Watercolour' A charming blend of dark and light pink. **D**
'White Dream' Snow white blooms which are long lasting. **FD**

Some Miniatures for the show bench

Avandel (pink-yellow peach blend)	Beauty Secret
Cupcake	Cecile Lens
Ko's Yellow	Jean Keneally
Magic Carrousel	Little Jackie
Pacesetter	Minnie Pearl
Starglo	Rise 'n Shine
	Starina

Some larger roses for the show bench

Alexander (medium-sized vermillion blooms. **D**)
Christian Dior (deep red, double blooms. **FD**)
Elina
Flamingo
French Lace
Gold Medal
Honour (white elegant blooms)
Julischka
Loving Memory
Margaret Merrill
Peace
Raspberry Ice
Satchmo
Sheer Bliss
Solitaire
The World

April Hamer
Auckland Metro
Diamond Jubilee
Double Delight
Esmeralda
Fragrant Cloud
Friesia
Grandpa Dickson
Iceberg
Lady Rose
Madame President
Marijke Koopman
Precious Platinum
Red Devil (very double red blooms)
Silver Lining
Sylvia
Trumpeter

Roses that Sam McGredy wishes he had raised

Double Delight
Fragrant Cloud
Iceberg

Elina
Friesia
Margaret Merrill

Favourite modern cultivars from Egmont Roses, New Plymouth, New Zealand

Hybrid teas: Aotearoa, Auckland Metro, Double Delight, Gold Medal, Loving Memory, Sheer Bliss, Whisky Mac (deep bronze buds, open gold. **F**).
Floribundas: Avalanche, French Lace, Friesia, Iceberg, Margaret Merrill, Old Port, Sexy Rexy.
Climbers: Compassion, Dublin Bay, Iceberg, Westerland.
Miniatures/Patio roses: Cupcake, Dorola, Kaikoura, Patio Jewel, Wanaka.

Favourite modern cultivars from Swanes Rose Nurseries, New South Wales, Australia

Hybrid teas: Aotearoa, Brandy, Double Delight, Fragrant Plum (deep lilac, edged rich purple), Gold Medal, Mr Lincoln (deep rich red), Oklahoma (deepest red/black, cuts well. **F**), Sheer Bliss, Touch of Class (coral pink, shaded salmon), Valerie Swane (ivory white. **F**)

Floribundas: Cherish (shell pinks blooms in profusion), French Lace, Friesia, Gay Princess (palest peach, classically shaped blooms), Lili Marlene (semi double, deep scented blooms. **FD**), Red Gold (large semi double blooms, edged red. **F**), Satchmo, Sunflare (profuse yellow blooms, short grower), White Simplicity (free flowering white, great for hedging. **D**).

Miniatures: Amorette (trusses of creamy white blooms. **F**), Buttons 'n' Bows (deepest pink double flowers), Guletta (elegant creamy yellow blooms), Holy Toledo, Kaikoura, Ko's Yellow, Mary Marshall, Petite Penny (pure white blooms, semi double in clusters), Queen Margarethe (clusters of soft pink blooms), Starina.

Climbers: Altissimo, Avon (large deep red blooms with classic shape), Blossom Time (cameo pink with china pink reverse), Golden Showers, Gwen Swane (small, shapely coral pink blooms), Iceberg, Papa Meilland, Peace, Princesse de Monaco (creamy white, edged carmine. **F**), Queen Elizabeth (carmine rose, pale pink double blooms. **F**).

The world's top favourite roses

1. Peace
2. Queen Elizabeth
3. Fragrant Cloud
4. Iceberg
5. Double Delight
6. Papa Meilland

11 Companion planting and inter-planting

And if you voz to see my rozis
As is a boon to all men's noziz,
You'd fall upon your back and scream -
'O Lawk, O Crikey! It's a dream!
Edward Lear

The practice of companion planting is as old as gardening itself. It is the growing of various plants close to others for their mutual benefit. This benefit can be physical, pertaining to the plants' health, or it may be aesthetic; plants that look good together.

For many years roses were grown in their own beds well away from other plants, against all the obvious rules of Nature. Happily, this style of rose gardening is now well on the outer and with the welcome return of the 'cottage garden' style roses are again taking their rightful place in the general garden scene, with other plants behind, among and under them. The rose is at its best in this type of planting, which more closely resembles the natural growth of all plants. No plant flourishes in Nature utterly separated from others and, in many ways, plants of different species can be of help to each other, providing support and shelter and attracting pollinating insects.

Do consider the combination of roses with other garden plants. In planning an integrated garden, attention needs to be paid to the growing requirements of the other plants as well as the roses, but if roses are to be the focal point, then consider their needs first and select plants that have similar nutritional needs. You will find there are some combinations that just won't work visually for you, so be sure to check the colours and sizes of the plants you include in your rose beds. Similarly, you would be unlikely to select bog plants like bog primulas or bulrushes, as their cultural needs are so diverse from those of roses.

There are, however, many plants that will live happily with roses. None of them are difficult to maintain and all will enhance the rose garden. This list of suggestions is by no means definitive or proscriptive; much of the fun of gardening consists of finding out for yourself what goes with what rather than slavishly following what someone else has done.

Experiment, observe, imagine, read, wander about other people's gardens, make lots of visits to garden centres to see what looks good in any given season and then make your own choices. But if your rose beds are looking bare and you need some ideas here are some suggestions for combinations that I find pleasing. These plants don't have to be dug up or tinkered with. They can be left to their own devices and the feedings that you give the roses will suit them, too.

Plants that may benefit roses

Garlic (*Allium sativum*)
Garlic is said to be one of the most effective insect repellents (especially for aphids), along with its close relatives, the chives. Garlic has attractive flowers with dense umbrels of greenish, white or pinkish flower heads. A few plants can be grown around the base of each rose as insect repellents, and garlic is also credited by many people as being of benefit in preventing black spot and mildew. The only way to prove this one way or the other is to try it yourself. You can of course, use the garlic cloves in cooking or blended with water as an aphid spray. Do, however, avoid trampling on the garlic plants, as the scent that arises will not be in the least rose-like!

Marigolds (*Calendula officinalis* or *Tagetes*)
Marigolds are helpful to have in any flower garden, as they tend to discourage nematodes, often called eelworms, which are parasitic on the roots of roses as well as other plants. Happily, marigolds don't have to be the rather brash orange colour that we all know, but can be found in pale pastel yellows and whites, some fragrant, which will blend easily with any garden colour scheme. They will germinate easily from seed and have a long flowering period.

Nicotiana (*Nicotiana* hybrids)
This plant is often said to be a natural insect repellent, with the added bonus of abundant flowers in shades from greenish white through

pink, mauve and red. The plant is a hardy annual (perennial in mild areas) which self-seeds readily, and the flowers give off a sweet fragrance, more so at night. Although nicotiana may help to discourage thrip and spider mites, aphids are fond of it, so check it when you are checking your roses for aphids.

Pyrethrum (*Tanacetum coccineum*)

A daisy-like plant that is the source of the well-known insecticide of the same name. It is not toxic to mammals. The flowers are small, white daisies which bloom from spring to autumn. Seed is easily germinated and the plants will self-seed if happy. Grown in mixed beds, pyrethrum will discourage insect pests.

Natural fertilisers for roses

Lucerne (*Medicago sativa*); clover (*Trifolium pratense*); and lupins (*Lupinus*) (and most other legumes) are of benefit to garden soil generally. They are usually sown before other plants, then dug in as a green manure before the flowering period, releasing beneficial levels of nitrogen to the soil from the nodules on their roots. All grow readily from seed and can best be used when you are preparing new beds for roses.

Living mulches

As mentioned in Chapter 2, roses benefit from having a layer of mulch material spread over the soil to insulate the roots from the heat of the summer sun and to give a cool root run. Mulching also suppresses weed growth and natural mulches eventually break down into humus, thus adding to the available nutrients in the soil. Compost, untreated sawdust, shredded garden waste and lawn clippings are often used as mulches. Black polythene is used, too, but is not a good choice as it prevents water and air circulation and the soil underneath can become very sour. It is much better to have a natural material as a mulch, or, even better, one that not only mulches but has its own flowers and perfume and complements the roses, too!

There are many plants that will fulfil the mulch function while also looking attractive and enhancing the whole appearance of the garden. Maintenance by weeding can eventually be eliminated and moisture evaporation will be reduced. The plants being used as a mulch will need little or no maintenance themselves, will reduce erosion in sloping beds, and will soften the outlines of beds, steps and paths. The following are all ground covers; low-growing plants that can be grown as a living mulch in rose beds, quickly covering bare earth before the weeds can get going and forming part of a natural, mutually beneficial community in the garden.

Acaena inermis purpurea
Ferny leaves that grow in purple, wine and red tonings. Matting habit with short stemmed seed heads that are long lasting.

Bell-flower (*Campanula*)
Perennial in a variety of colours. Plant close together for mass effect. Seeds easily in most situations. Lots of showy flowers in blues and white. Use low-growing varieties for ground cover and the taller varieties as superb complementary plants for roses.

Ground Morning Glory (*Convolvulus mauretanicus*)
Perennial of suckering type which will spill over banks with trails of mauve flowers. Nowhere near as rampant as its climbing relative, which is most often seen running amok in neglected gardens.

Lobelia (*Lobelia inflata*)
Annual. Will self-seed almost anywhere and will cover itself with small blue flowers which, according to variety, can range from pale baby blue to deep royal blue.

Love in a Mist (*Nigella*)
Another self-seeding annual with white, pink or blue flowers and ferny, lush foliage. Taller growing than lobelia, it is more suited to sheltered areas and a produces a mass of very pickable flowers.

Penny-royal (*Mentha pulegium*)
A very aromatic, low-growing ground cover which forms a thick mat and spreads over edges and on to paths, where it can be walked on, releasing the aroma. Also good in the lawn for the same reason. Grows from seed or from rooted slips.

Periwinkle (*Vinca minor*)
Extremely useful in shaded areas such as under climbing roses. The periwinkles come in a variety of pastel colours, spread by suckering and will cover large areas very rapidly. Flowers are usually single and

will appear throughout the year. Select only *V. minor*, as other varieties can become rampant.

Snow in Summer (*Cerastium tomentosum*)
Stem-rooting type. Quick spreading silvery grey foliage and innumerable tiny white flowers in summer. Propagates easily from cuttings or divisions. Select the less rampant C. *columnae*.

Sweet Alice (*Alyssum maritimum*)
A self-seeding annual that creates a mass of low-growing, sweetly scented white, pink or mauve flowers which will smother the ground.

Thyme (*Thymus*)
Thyme comes in many varieties, most low-growing and some of which will spill their aromatic foliage and tiny flowers over paths and garden edges. A wealth of different fragrances can be found. Thymes are tough little plants which can be propagated by division. Perfect for small areas, even pots and tubs.

Violets (*Viola* sp.)
Many colours, all ground-hugging, and many will flower for most of the year. Particularly useful for covering the ground rapidly is the Tasmanian native violet (*V. hederacea*), which spreads from self-rooting shoots and bears small mauve and white flowers all year. If you prefer the more scented varieties, look for the recently released series of 'Wylde Green Cottage' scented violets. Pansies, of the same family as violets, are also good for covering the ground and will self-seed if happy. Highly recommended is Heartsease (*V. tricolour*), which, like that well-known admirer of violets, Napoleon Bonaparte, will always return in the spring.

Wild Strawberry (*Fragaria japonica*)
A valuable matting plant which spreads generously, sometimes too generously perhaps, in all directions. Strawberry-like flowers and fruits which are sadly tasteless, although blackbirds covet them.

Ground cover roses
There are numerous rose cultivars that will obligingly cover the ground underneath their taller growing relatives. Their culture is the same as

for other cultivars, and many can be grown in tubs or hanging baskets as well. Some recommended ground cover roses are:

'Green Ice' Pale pink buds opening to double white flowers edged with green.

'Nozomi' Vigorous. Pale pink buds and single flowers in spring.

'Red Cascade' Small, deep red blooms on long canes which will arch in all directions.

'Snow Carpet' A vigorous grower with creamy white double flowers in spring.

'The Fairy' Larger growing than the above, 'The Fairy' is one of the world's most popular roses. Soft pink, double flowers that repeat all season in broad sprays. Great for covering unsightly tree stumps.

There are also some Old-fashioned roses that can be used as ground covers, but these tend to be for very large areas. With all ground covers, some initial weeding may be necessary until the plants become established. Layers of dampened newspaper over areas of bare soil will help to prevent weed seed germination until the ground cover plants take over this function for themselves.

Plants that complement roses

All of the plants listed here will grow happily with roses. Their presence will visually enhance the rose beds and they will thrive on the same nourishment that is given to the roses.

Australian Mint Bush (*Prosanthera*)
A profuse flowering shrub bearing tiny flowers in pinks and mauves. Ideal in hot, dry areas. The foliage is freshly aromatic.

Baby's Breath (*Gypsophyla*)
Fine, delicate foliage and starry white or pink flowers, much used by florists as a foil to other flowers. Perennial and annual types are available and will self-seed if happy.

Bishop's Flower (*Ammi majus*)
Lacy white flowers on tall stems on a plant that resembles Queen Anne's Lace, but flowers for longer, often through till autumn. Annual.

Blue Marguerite (*Felicia*)
Shrubby perennial from Africa. Sky-blue daisy flowers which will continue for a long period if dead-headed. Cut back annually or re-grow from cuttings.

Catmint (*Nepeta mussinii*)
Spikes of lavender blue flowers rising from a haze of foliage which is gently mint-scented. Plant 'en masse' for best effect.

Chamomile (*Anthemis nobilis*)
Very low-growing, with a rich aroma from the foliage when crushed. Bears small white flowers and mossy foliage. The variety 'Treneague' (non-flowering) can also be used as a lawn substitute which is fragrant and never needs mowing.

Common Sage (*Salvia officinalis*)
The leaves and flowers are scented. Flower colour varies from white through pinks and purples. Flowers appear from early summer to autumn. Easily grown from seed or cuttings.

Coreopsis
Often dismissed due to its rather bright yellow tones, there is a soft lemon variety, C. *verticillata* 'Moonbeam', which has light, fine foliage, is extremely hardy and has a long flowering period.

Cornflower (*Centaurea*)
Buttonhole-sized flowers in rich blue or pink; lovely for small posies. Will self-seed if happy.

Day Lily (*Hemerocallis*)
Leaves are rush-like and the big flowers resembling lilies will bloom over a long period producing new flowers each day. Colours range from cream through orange to deep red. The plants are bulbous and form clumps.

Delphinium (*Ranunculacea*)
Wonderful for background planting. Tall spires of flowers on long stems in summer. Self-seeding in a variety of colours, sometimes bicolours, all of which will blend with roses. Plant in groups of one colour for best effect. Some taller varieties may need staking. Dwarf

varieties are available. Perennial delphiniums are also suitable for growing with roses.

Foxgloves (*Digitalis*)
Tall growing spires of finger-sized tubular flowers. Leaves are downy and silvery green. Flowers come in colours from white through pinks and apricots to deep purple and maroon, often with contrasting colour dotted on the throats. Happy in partial shade and will self-seed. Recommended varieties are *D. purpurea alba*, a famous white foxglove found in old gardens, and *D. viridiflora*, a rare, lime green variety.

Geranium (*Geraniaceae*) Crane's Bill
Delicate, lacy leaves with open flowers from white through pale pink and mauve. Many varieties are available, some with variegated leaves. The flowers are unobtrusive, unlike the larger flowered pelargoniums. Highly recommended is *G. traversii*, often grown as a rockery plant. White flowers sometimes to pale pink, with greyish green leaves.

Granny Bonnets (*Aquilegia*)
Graceful nodding flowers, the epitome of the cottage garden. Foliage is tufty and resembles maidenhair fern. Old varieties are available along with some new hybrids. Recommended are *A. caerulea* 'Crystal', a pure white, and *A. vulgaris* 'Nora Barlow' with double spurless flowers suffused with reddish pink and green. Dwarf varieties are also available in many colours, and doubles are highly desirable.

Hebe
There are hundreds of varieties of this compact plant which bears panicles of flowers above grey-green leaves. Flowers range in colour from white through pink and mauve.

Hollyhock (*Althaea*)
Very tall perennial or biennial up to 3 m in height. Tall spires of flowers which may be single or double and in a variety of colours. Recommended is the single black which is invaluable as an accent plant, and the Charters double series with glorious peony-like flowers from white through pinks and scarlets to maroon.

Iris (*Iridaceae*)

The genus comprises around 200 species, which are bulbous or rhizomatous types. The foliage is spiky, lush and greenish-grey. Flowers are large and generally in soft colours. Irises grow happily with roses, and as they generally flower in September before the roses start, they give some substance to rose beds when the new rose growth is just getting under way. Recommended cultivars are 'Wedgewood', a classic sky-blue; 'Prof. Blau', ultramarine violet blue; 'White Beauty', snow white with a yellow blotch; and *I. sibirica* in many colours.

Lady's Mantle (*Alchemilla mollis*)

Perennial that covers itself with lime green flowers and looks wonderful with Old-fashioned roses.

Lavatera (*Malvaceaea*)

Select perennial types which are tall growing plants related to hollyhocks. *L.* 'Barnsley' is a new variety smothering itself with pale pink flowers. Look also for annual varieties like *L.* 'Mont Blanc', growing to just 60 cm with pure white flowers all summer, and *L.* 'Silver Cup', growth habit as for 'Mont Blanc', but with glowing pink flowers.

Lavender (*Lavandula*)

There are many varieties of this popular plant which is a 'natural' for growing with roses. Lavenders come in shades of mauve/purple, but white, pink and green varieties are available. Long spikes of fragrant flowers and foliage on bushes up to a metre in height. Perfect in hedges or as a taller border plant.

Libertia (*Iridaceae*)

Perennials of rhizomatous habit and iris-like foliage. New Zealand native species are *L.caerulescens* with pale blue flowers and *L. grandiflora* with white flowers on lightly branched stems.

Lithodora diffusa

A prostrate plant with bright blue flowers in spring. The plant is of shrubby growth and can be trimmed back after flowering. Recommended cultivar is 'Heavenly Blue'.

Mignonette (*Reseda odorata*)

An annual or biennial with musk-scented flowers in tufts on tall spikes. Flowers are cuttable and range from cream through yellowish brown.

Nemesia

Short-growing edging plant often used as a ground cover. An enormous variety of colours from cream through gold to scarlet, and including a blue, dwarf variety. Nemesias may be annual or perennial.

Parahebes

These are shrubby plants with neat foliage habit and showy flowers. They are related to the larger and better known Hebes. *P. catarractae* grows to 30 cm and has summer flowers of white, blotched with purple. *P. lyallii* is a tiny 10 cm in height, of prostrate habit and bears pale lilac flowers. *P. olsenii* has pink flowers over bronzy foliage and is perfect for nooks and crannies among rockery edging.

Pinks (*Dianthus*)

Drought resistant, profuse-flowering plants with a low growth habit. Flowers are often heavily scented and range in colour from white through pinks to maroon with some bi-colours. Recommended are 'Miss Sinkins', white and heavily scented; 'Maiden Pink', sweetly scented pink through red flowers; 'Cheddar Pink', with fragrant single pink flowers; 'Counterpart', cerise blooms with darker markings; and 'Far Cry', with a strong clove fragrance and pinky mauve flowers.

Penstemon

There are some lovely hybrids of this genus that come in a good range of colours from near white through pinks, crimson and purple. Showy flowers on perennial plants that enjoy full sun. Some of the best are the Alpine penstemons especially *P. heterophyllus* 'True Blue' which is of sprawling habit, but the flowers are produced on upright stems in a clear, deep blue.

P. procerus has mauve/purple flowers with yellow beards, and *P. humilis* forms a low mat from which rise stems of electric blue flowers with golden beards. All are prolific flowerers.

Plantain Lily (*Hosta*)

These are mainly grown for their foliage which contrasts beautifully with roses. Various leaf forms and colours are available. Mauve, bell-like flowers on tall stems. Hostas relish shade and so should be planted beneath taller roses.

Primroses (*Primula vulgaris*)
Unlike the ubiquitous polyanthus, which seem to grow bigger and brighter with each passing year, the wild primrose is always pastel coloured and unobtrusive. It is a ground-hugger with small, delicate flowers forming mid-winter to summer. A lovely, much neglected plant that is the epitome of spring. Look also for *P. vulgaris* in blue or white as well as the familiar pale lemon, and some double forms are available, too.

Queen Anne's Lace (*Anthriscus sylvestrus*)
Ferny foliage and masses of tiny white flowers in panicles. A biennial or perennial which flowers from late spring to summer.

Rosemary (*Rosemarinus officinalis*)
Aromatic perennial shrub with woody branches. Flowers are small, usually pale blue, but sometimes white to light lavender, and appear in late spring through summer. The foliage is a deep green. Upright and prostrate forms are available.

Swamp Musk (*Mazus radicans*)
A delightful, flowering ground-hugger for moist areas under roses. Small white flowers and densely packed foliage distinguishes this plant which will spread to cover a large area.

Winter Rose (*Helleborus*)
Low-growing plants which enjoy shaded places under roses, and will benefit from the humus enriched soil. Tall stems will produce unusual flowers from green through white and pink to purple. Slow to establish, but worth the effort and hardy once established. Helleborus flower in winter when few other flowers are about. Best 'en masse'.

Yarrow (*Achillea*)
Easily grown perennial with masses of summer flowers in white, yellow, pink and red.

For those keen gardeners seeking some of the more unusual and difficult to obtain plants listed, several mail order plant specialists who advertise in gardening magazines will provide inspirational catalogues with many more plants suitable for growing with roses.

12 Using your roses

Gather ye rosebuds while ye may,
Old time is still a-flying;
And this same flower that smiles today
Tomorrow will be dying.

Robert Herrick

Roses as cut flowers

When you are growing roses, you want to use them in every possible way. The show of roses in the garden is a joy, not only for the gardener, but also for visitors and passers by, but you will want to pick blooms too. As with the growing of roses, there are some tips to be learned in order to have rose blooms looking as good in the house as they do on the plants. Experienced flower arrangers can teach all of us some of the 'tricks of the trade'.

The vase life of cut roses can be prolonged with care. Hybrid teas, such as those favoured by exhibitors, will hold their shape better than cultivars with just a few petals, and floribundas will last well, too.

Pick the flowers in the early morning or evening if possible. Always cut to a five-leaflet leaf every time, for the sake of the bush, and don't cut stems longer than you need to, as this will mean a longer time before the next bloom appears on the bush. Take with you into the garden a bucket or other deep container filled with tepid water (tepid water is taken up more readily than cold water) and immediately plunge each flower into the container as it is taken from the bush; having the water right up to the calyx (the base of the flower). Then, holding the stem under water, re-cut each stem, just a few millimetres higher. This will prevent an 'air lock' which may stop the uptake of water by the stem, so this re-cutting will prolong vase life for the flowers.

When you have sufficient blooms for your needs, take the container inside and place it somewhere cool for a few hours or overnight before arranging the blooms in containers. Some people add glucose or glycerine to the water, some add an aspirin, or a drop or two of bleach, or one of the commercial preparations available for helping cut flowers to last longer. The aim of all these additives is the same, to provide a little nourishment for the flowers and to prevent the entry of bacteria at the cut on the stem.

When you have arranged the roses, keep the vases topped up with water. Removing a little each day and replacing it with fresh water will help, too. Roses will droop fast in a hot, dry atmosphere, so a high level of water in the vase will help to maintain humidity. Keep the vase out of direct sunlight and the roses will last much longer.

Roses in floral art

Mainly Hybrid tea-type roses are recommended for floral art, as they tend to hold their shape and freshness for longer than the older roses. If you plan on getting into floral art, it is useful to have several plants of each cultivar so that you are always assured of enough blooms for your needs. When using roses for floral work, it is important to cut and prepare the blooms long before you want to arrange them. To help them to last longer, plunge the stems into water that has just boiled, and hold them there for about nine seconds before leaving them to have a good soak in tepid water.

Hybrid teas are also selected for mixed arrangements because the single flowers are more easily managed than clusters of flowers that you would get on Floribundas. Their high pointed centres make for contrast in the arrangements as most other flowers open flat. It is helpful to remove the thorns before beginning to arrange the flowers.

Pretty in pink

'Madame President' A lovely soft pink rose and a great favourite with arrangers, as well as being a good garden rose. It has perfume, repeats quickly and can be used for all occasions; from a bridesmaid's bouquet to a posy bowl. It can be teamed with pink King proteas and silver Astelia leaves for a larger design.

'Pink Flamingo' This rose has excellent keeping qualities, long stems and shapely blooms and is often used with accessories from driftwood to your best silver.

'Queen Elizabeth' Another good pink that can be used for large arrangements such as pedestal displays.

Other favoured pinks are: 'Pink Parfait' (satin pink blended with cream. D) , 'Sylvia', 'First Love', 'The Fairy', and the climbing 'Pink

Sparrieshoop' (old-fashioned shrub rose with single apricot pink flowers. **F**).

Wedding day roses
The white **'Francis Phoebe'** is the best true white for a bride dressed in pure white, as many of the other whites photograph a distinct cream against today's stark white dress fabrics. **'Pascali'**, however, is a must for the bride in cream. Flowers for the church could include **'Virgo'** (smallish bloom, purest white), **'Honour'**, **'Margaret Merrill'**, **'True Love'** (near white, flushed pink) and sprays of **'Iceberg'**.

Red roses
For Valentine's Day or for any time you want to say , 'I love you'. Also for Christmas flower arrangements. Varieties could include: **'Bull's Red'**(free flowering with dark red blooms), **'Loving Memory'**, **'National Trust'** (medium-sized crimson scarlet blooms), **'Avenue Red'** (dark red blooms. **D**), **'Josephine Bruce'** (deep crimson velvet blooms) and the climber **'Dublin Bay'**.

For impact at the rose show
Once you get past the thorns, the brilliant orange red of **'Prominent'** is sure to get attention, and **'Alexander'**, **'Lady Rose'** and **'Fragrant Cloud'** will also delight those who love these vibrant colours. .

Yellow roses
To bring the sunshine indoors try **'Gold medal'**, **'Mabella'** (deep yellow centred, fading to petal edges) and **'Landora'** (an unfading yellow of medium size). These are all good yellows with long stems and a pleasing shape.

For something different
Try the glorious parchment colour of **'Julia's Rose'**, which, though exceptionally beautiful, is often a little shy of flowers. Team it up with buds of **'Cream Delight'** (deepest cream high centred blooms) for a real talking point.

Softer tones for a gentler look
Try **'Vienna Woods'** (big blooms of soft salmon pink), **'Dolce Vita'** (deepest salmon blooms of perfect form), **'Sexy Rexy'**, and **'Nitouche'**,

a lovely, long lasting apricot centred rose renowned for its keeping qualities.

Miniature roses and spray roses have become more popular and are useful for wedding bouquets. They blend well with the larger roses for table arrangements, baskets and posies.

Flowers that will blend with roses for floral art work are carnations, gladioli, gypsophylla, snapdragons, foxgloves, astilbe, statice, watsonias, ericas, nigella, larkspur, flax, ivy leaves, conifers, copper beach leaves, geranium leaves and Queen Anne's Lace ... and that's just for a start!

Exhibiting roses in shows

When you visit rose shows, you may well come to the conclusion that the roses in your garden are every bit as good as the ones that have won all the prizes, and, of course, your conclusion would be correct. Those prize winning blooms are from exactly the same cultivars that we all grow! You don't need to be an 'expert' to show roses, but some advice from frequent, successful exhibitors will be a great help if you are showing roses for the first few times.

If you are a member of a rose society, there is usually a monthly competition that you can enter, and you can learn a great deal from observing the way roses are shown there, and by watching and talking to the exhibitors. You can ask the judges there for tips about what they look for in roses for exhibition. Most exhibitors will be happy to help you when they realise that you are interested.

In shows, all roses are judged under three headings:
1. Form
2. Substance and Freshness
3. Stem, Balance and Foliage

Form may vary with different types of exhibits, but substance and freshness are the same for all roses. Substance refers to the texture of the petals, and freshness refers to the colour and sheen on the petals.

Definitions of classes for showing

The following description of guidelines for judges and exhibitors may change slightly between rose societies and the judging standards are subject to constant review.

A Decorative Bloom is from one quarter to half open, having well formed petals of good substance, arranged to produce a refined shape of more slender proportions than in the fuller 'Exhibition' type. The flower should still be long and narrow at the base with several outer petals opening, rather than just past the bud stage.

An Exhibition Bloom is one which is half to three quarters open, has ample petals of good substance free from blemish that are symmetrically and gracefully arranged to form a circular outline around a well formed centre. They should be balanced on a stem which is neither weak nor coarse in proportion to the bloom. Foliage must be clean, healthy and well arranged.

A Fully Open Bloom must be past the three quarters open stage and the outline circular. The petals should show crispness and lustre with no tendency to be droopy or floppy.

Other Classes There are also in most show schedules, classes for miniature roses, stems for roses with not more than three flowers, four or more flowers open, and classes for vases of blooms and bowls of blooms. Some shows also have a special class for locally raised seedling roses raised by the exhibitor, and there are usually classes for Old-fashioned roses, too.

Judging

Judging is a complex process, and judges will have had to study and pass exams before they are let loose in a show, so you can be sure that they know what they're looking for. Showing roses can be a fascinating offshoot of your interest in roses. It can also be rather addictive, and can get you to the nail biting stage. The challenge here is in seeing if you can prepare your roses for show as well as experienced exhibitors; you already know that you grow them as well!

Exhibiting is said to be part art, part craft and part competitive sport, and you will enjoy the company of other exhibitors once all the exhibits are arranged and you are awaiting judging. Judging can become so fascinating that you decide you want to become qualified as a judge yourself and see how it feels from the other side of the exhibiting bench.

Rose cultivars that very frequently win prizes at shows are listed in Chapter 10, so you might like to try some of those for a start, if exhibiting interests you.

Other ways to use roses

It seems a pity to waste all those rose petals when the flowers have faded, so try some of these recipes to keep the spirit of the roses with you all year. In most of the recipes, fresh petals are best, but for pot pourri, faded petals are quite satisfactory. Any fragrant roses are suitable for all the recipes, and the colour and fragrance of the roses will affect the resulting colour and fragrance of the finished product.

Dry pot pourri
Petals of fragrant cultivars should be thoroughly dried until they are papery. Spread them out thinly on newspaper for a few days in warm weather. Mix with any combination of scented leaves and flowers that you have in the garden. Some inclusions could be the flowers of stocks, honeysuckle, jasmine, pinks, carnations, and wallflowers. Use the flowers and foliage of lavender, rosemary, thymes of all kinds, and the leaves of scented geraniums and pelargoniums, lemon balm, pine-apple sage, spearmint, eau de cologne mint, pennyroyal, bergamot, southernwood, lemon grass and chamomile. The drying process is hastened if you cut up the leaves and stalks before setting them to dry. You can add dry material as the season progresses, and provided the mixture is not left uncovered for too long, the fragrance will remain for up to two years.

When mixed, store in airtight jars and use the mixture to fill pot pourri jars of your choice. You can also make fabric sachets filled with the mixture for wardrobes and linen cupboards and as unique gifts for friends. Mix the flowers and foliage in amounts so that one fragrance does not dominate.

Moist pot pourri
This will retain its fragrance longer as it contains fixatives of salt and/or orris root, the dried and powdered root of the iris *Germanica*. Gather and dry the flowers and foliage as above, spreading layers of the dried mixture in a wide-necked jar, sprinkling each layer with a mixture of sea salt, common salt and/or orris root (usually available at pharmacies).

Make the fixative layer about 6 mm deep, then continue to add petals and foliage and fixative layers until the jar is full. Cover the jar and keep in a dark place until you want to use the contents. To make the mix into a truly unique pot pourri, add ground cloves, grated citrus rind, cinnamon and allspice and leave overnight. Then add a few drops of essential oils of geranium, bergamot or lavender and leave closed in the container for a few weeks more. The essential oils can also be used as a 'reviver' for pot pourri that is beginning to lose its fragrance. A few teaspoons of brandy will also revive a fading mixture.

Rose vinegar
Use deep red petals, cutting off the white part at the base of each petal. Dry the petals, then put them in white vinegar in a closed bottle in the sun. The vinegar will gradually take on the colour and some of the fragrance of the petals. Remove the petals occasionally and replace them with fresh ones. Strain out the last of the petals and store the vinegar in clear, closed bottles. For gift giving, a miniature rosebud on a long stem can be inserted into the bottle or tied on the outside.

Rose petal jelly
Simmer some chopped apples, including the peel, and add a good handful of red rose petals to every 500 ml of water. After simmering, strain off the juice on to another handful of petals, discarding the puree. After a day or two, add more petals and 350 g of sugar to every 500 ml of juice. Bring to the boil quickly and simmer until a little will set in a saucer. Remove from heat and add the strained juice of half a lemon to each 500 ml of jelly. Strain through muslin and pour into jars which must be closed at once.

Rose hip jelly
Top-and-tail well-ripened hips, cover, bring to boil and simmer with 750 ml of water to 900 g of hips. Simmer 30 to 40 minutes or until the hips become soft. Squash the pulp through a wire strainer, then through muslin. Let it drip through the muslin, as forcing can make the jelly cloudy; let it drip overnight if necessary. Add 450 g of sugar and half a teaspoon of Tartaric Acid to every 500 ml of juice. Return to heat and simmer until a little jelly dropped on a saucer will set. Pour into jars and close at once.

Rose Scented Ink
Bring half a cup of tightly packed petals and half a cup of cold water to the boil and simmer gently with cover on for 20 to 30 minutes, not allowing the water to completely evaporate, but it will partially disappear and the remainder turn a brownish colour. Strain and allow to cool, then add the liquid to a bottle of ink and keep capped. You can also

perfume ink with lavender, rosemary or any other scented flowers or foliage in the same way.

Rose scented notepaper
Store some notepaper with your dried rose petals or with pot pourri to give it a light fragrance.

Crystallised rose petals
Beat the white of an egg into a foam with half a teaspoon of cold water. Dip rose petals into it one at a time, then dip into castor sugar. Place petals, well separated, on waxed paper in the sun to dry. The crystallised petals can be stored in an airtight jar to be used when you want them for decorating cakes or desserts. Use some to decorate the next recipe; a delicious and special dessert.

Rose syllabub
Finely grate the rind of a lemon and stir together with its juice and four tablespoons of rosé wine and 100 g of castor sugar, then leave overnight. Next day, gently stir in 250 ml of cream and the tiniest drop of red colouring. Then beat the mixture till it resembles whipped cream and spoon it into individual glasses. Decorate with crystallised petals and / or strips of crystallised Angelica.

Rose beads
Little girls love these! For a perfumed necklace, mix one and a half to two cups of plain flour with four tablespoons of common salt and mix in just enough water to make thick paste. Mix in three cups of finely chopped scented rose petals and about 12 drops of Rose Geranium oil. You could add a drop or two of red colouring if you like as the dried beads will be somehat lighter in colour than the wet mixture.

Form into small beads and string on to fine wire to dry. Fuse wire or florists wire is suitable. When the beads have dried, they can be threaded on to nylon cord. If after a time the beads lose their fragrance, you can roll them about in a jar with a few more drops of the oil. Remember to dry them thoroughly again if you do this.

Rose cologne
Soak half a cup of fresh rose petals with half a cup of isopropyl alcohol, which is sometimes available from pharmacists. If you can't get it, use Vodka instead. Keep in a closed jar for about a week and strain before use. You can make the cologne more interesting by adding an infusion of citrus peel, and other scented herbs like mint, lemon verbena, etc.,

before straining through cheesecloth. The strained out petals and herbs can go into your pot pourri mix when they are dried.

Rosewater

Mix 25 ml of rose oil with 850 ml of isopropyl alcohol and shake thoroughly. Leave to stand for about a week, shaking occasionally. Pour the liquid into small bottles and cap tightly. You do the same for lavender water or any other strongly scented or aromatic plants.

Spicy perfume

Use a cup of rosewater, 8 g of bruised cloves (not powdered as this will cause cloudiness), one bay leaf, and a cup of white or wine vinegar. Bring to the boil and simmer gently to reduce the amount of liquid, finally adding water to return to the original amount of fluid. Strain and keep in closed jars for a month or two before pouring into small bottles and capping tightly.

There are lots more uses for your rose petals and hips. You are only limited by your imagination. For tea with a rose fragrance, add a cup of dried, perfumed rose petals to a packet of tea. Make in the usual way, but leave to draw just a minute longer so that the rose fragrance will permeate the brew.

You can add rosewater to soaps and to body powders using corn-flower or orris root as a base, and, of course, the heps and petals can be made into a very pleasant wine. Allen Paterson suggests that 'this should be drunk by keen rosarians in winter as they read through the catalogues and order ever more bushes from the growers.'[5] He may well have a good point there, but do get your order in long before winter if you're after something special!

Glossary

Bare root roses. Rose bought without any soil around their roots; usually in plastic bags and usually available only in winter.

Basal shoot/water shoot. A shoot growing from above the bud union, forming the framework for subsequent years' growth.

Bud union/bud head. The place at which the scion is budded on to the rootstock.

Budding. The method of inserting growth buds from a wanted cultivar into the bark of an understock.

Clone. a plant propagated from tissue of the parent, i.e., through tissue culture, layering or by cutting.

Cultivar. Short for 'cultivated variety.' A variety of rose raised in cultivation. Not a species rose.

Damping off. A fungus disease that causes seedlings to wither and die. Spray soil with fungicide to prevent or spray with a weak solution of potassium permanganate (Condy's crystals).

Dead-heading. Removing spent flower heads to encourage new growth.

Die back. The slow dying back of a cane, usually from a pruning cut.

Eye/budding eye. Small amount of tissue growing between the stem and a leaf. The part used to bud on to rootstock.

Friable (of soil). Able to be worked. Rule of thumb about friability is that if some is squeezed in the hand, it will retain its shape when released, but still crumble when touched.

Hep/hip. Rose seed pods, usually yellow, orange, red when ripened.

Heeling in. Temporary planting of roses.

Mulch. A layer of material laid over beds to conserve moisture, reduce summer temperatures and suppress weed growth. Can be inorganic, e.g., polythene, but more often organic, e.g., bark, compost, sawdust, seaweed, grass clippings, etc.

Own root roses. Cloned plants grown from cuttings, tissue culture or layering. Not budded on to understock.

Propagation. Any method if increasing the numbers of plants.

Repeat flowering/recurrent/remontant. The ability of a cultivar to flower again in the same season after the first flush of bloom.

Rootstock. See understock.

Scion. The cultivar which is budded on to the rootstock.

Species. A wild rose; one not raised through cultivation; not a hybrid.

Sport. A mutation; a shoot that is different in some way from the parent plant. Growth eyes or cuttings from the mutant shoot may be used to propagate the sport.

Sucker. Growth arising from below the bud union. In budded plants, the sucker will be from the rootstock, and should be removed; in cloned plants, the sucker is of the same cultivar as the clone, and can be used for propagation or allowed to grow, making a bushier plant.

Systemic (of fungicides and pesticides). Able to be absorbed by the leaves and translocated to all parts of the plant, thus remaining effective for longer.

Understock. The plant on to which the wanted cultivar is budded. Understocks are selected for their vigour and disease resistance.

Variety. In rose terms, this means the same as cultivar.

Endnotes

1, 2   Austin, David, *The Heritage of the Rose*, Anitue Collectors Club Suffolk, United Kingdom, 1988.
3   Griffiths, Trevor, *My World of Old Roses*, Vol 2, Whitcoulls, New Zealand, 1986.
4   Paterson, Allen, *The History of the Rose*, Collins, United Kingdom, 1983.
5   *Ibid.*

Bibliography and further reading

Austin, David, *The Heritage of the Rose*, Antique Collectors' Club, 1988

Australia and New Zealand Complete Book of Gardening, Paul Hamlyn, 1977

Bell, R.J., *The Amateur Rose Breeder's Guide*, Dandenong Printing Co. Ltd., [no date]

Dann, Christine, *Cottage Gardening in New Zealand*, Allen and Unwin, 1990

Eagle, Dawn and Barry, *Miniature Roses*, Collins, 1985

Fisher, John, *The Companion to Roses*, Penguin Books, 1986

Gibson, Michael, *The Rose Gardens of England*, Collins, 1988

Griffiths, Trevor, *My World of Old Roses*, Vol 1, Whitcoulls, 1987
    My World of Old Roses, Vol 2, Whitcoulls, 1986
    A Celebration of Old Roses, Penguin Books, 1990

Harkness, Jack, *The Rose*, McGraw Hill, 1979

Hayward, Margaret, *A New Zealand Guide to Miniature Roses*, Grantham House, 1988

Holyoake, C.V., *Roses: Cultural Handbook*, National Rose Society, 1982

McGredy, Sam, *Look to the Rose*, Bateman, 1986

Paterson, Allen, *The History of the Rose*, Collins, 1983

Redgrove, Hugh (ed.), *A New Zealand Handbook of Bulbs and Perennials*, Godwit Press, 1991

Riotte, Louise, *Roses Love Garlic*, Doubleday, 1989

Squire, David, et al., *The Scented Garden*, Doubleday, 1989

Thomas, A.S., *Knowing, Growing and Showing Roses*, Macmillan, 1975

Wyatt, L.A., *The Complete Rosarian*, Hodder and Stoughton, 1971

Index

Index of rose names